BLACK LEGACY PRESS™
WWW.BLACKLEGACYPRESS.ORG

Slave Narratives

VOLUME VII
KENTUCKY NARRATIVES

By
United States.
Work Projects Administration

Copyright © 2023 by BLACKLEGACYPRESS.ORG

All rights reserved. No part of this publication may be reproduced or transmitted in any form or by any means electronic or mechanical, including information storage and retrieval systems without permission in writing from the publisher, except for student research using the appropriate citations.

ISBN: 978-1-63652-224-1

SLAVE NARRATIVES

A Folk History of Slavery in the United States.
From Interviews with Former Slaves

**UNITED STATES.
WORK PROJECTS ADMINISTRATION**

TYPEWRITTEN RECORDS PREPARED BY
THE FEDERAL WRITERS' PROJECT
1936-1938
ASSEMBLED BY
THE LIBRARY OF CONGRESS PROJECT
WORK PROJECTS ADMINISTRATION
FOR THE DISTRICT OF COLUMBIA
SPONSORED BY THE LIBRARY OF
CONGRESS

WASHINGTON 1941

VOLUME VII
KENTUCKY NARRATIVES

Prepared by
The Federal Writers' Project of
The Works Progress Administration
For the State of Kentucky

CONTENTS

Dan Bogie 1
George Henderson 5
Harriet Mason 9
Bert Mayfield 13
Will Oats 19
Belle Robinson 23
Edd Shirley 25
Wes Woods 27
Ann Gudgel 31
Mrs. Heyburn 33
George Scruggs 35
Harriet Mason 39
Rev. John R. Cox 43
Mrs. Duncan 47
Mrs. Elizabeth Alexander 51
Amelia Jones 55
Jenny McKee 61
Susan Dale Sanders 65
John Anderson 69
Joana Owens 71
Martha J. Jones 73
Charlie Richmond 75
George Dorsey 81
Annie B. Boyd 89

Kate Billingsby	93
Nannie Eaves	95
Mary Wright	97
Sophia Word	103
Carl F. Hall	107
Mandy Gibson	115
Scott Mitchell	119
A Bill of Sale	121
Nancy Austin	123
Robert Mullins	125
Mayme Nunnelley	127
Gladys Robertson	133
Edd Shirley	137
Peter Bruner	141
Easter Sudie Campbell	145
Uncle Dick	151
Annie Morgan	163
Cora Torian	165
Mary Wooldridge	169
CALDWELL	175
Tinie Force and Elvira Lewis	179
LAWRENCE	185
LESLIE	187
GARRARD	189
WEBSTER	191
CALDWELL	193
ANDERSON	195

KNOX 197
CLARK 199
CASEY 201
CHRISTIAN 203
HOPKINS 207
MARTIN 209

GARRARD COUNTY. EX-SLAVE STORIES.
(ELIZA ISON) [HW: KY 9]
INTERVIEW WITH DAN BOGIE:

DAN BOGIE

Uncle Dan tells me "he was born May 5, 1858 at the Abe Wheeler place near Spoonsville, now known as Nina, about nine miles due east from Lancaster. Mother, whose name was Lucinda Wheeler, belonged to the Wheeler family. My father was a slave of Dan Bogie's, at Kirksville, in Madison County, and I was named for him. My mother's people were born in Garrard County as far as I know. I had one sister, born in 1860, who is now dead, and is buried not far from Lancaster. Marse Bogie owned about 200 acres of land in the eastern section of the county, and as far as I can remember there were only four slaves on the place. We lived in a one-room cabin, with a loft above, and this cabin was an old fashioned one about hundred yards from the house. We lived in one room, with one bed in the cabin. The one bed was an old fashioned, high post corded bed where my father and mother slept. My sister and me slept in a trundle bed, made like the big bed except the posts were made smaller and was on rollers, so it could be rolled under the big bed. There was also a cradle, made of a wooden box, with rockers nailed on, and my mother told me that she rocked me in that cradle when I was a baby. She used to sit and sing in the evening. She carded the wool and spun yarn on the old spinning wheel. My grandfather was a slave of Talton Embry, whose farm joined the Wheeler farm. He made shingles with a steel drawing knife, that had a wooden handle. He made these shingles in Mr. Embry's yard. I do not remember my grandmother, and I didn't have to work in slave days, because my mother and father did all the work except the heavy farm work. My Mistus used to give me my winter clothes. My shoes were called brogans. My old master had shoes made. He would put my foot on the floor and mark around it for the measure of my shoes.

Most of the cooking was in an oven in the yard, over the bed of coals. Baked possum and ground hog in the oven, stewed rabbits, fried fish and fired bacon called "streaked meat" all kinds of vegetables, boiled cabbage, pone corn bread, and sorghum molasses. Old folks would drink coffee, but chillun would drink milk, especially butter milk.

Old master would call us about 4 o'clock, and everybody had to get up and go to "Starring"[TR:?]. Old Marse had about 30 or 40 sugar trees which were tapped, in February. Elder spiles were stuck in the taps for the water to drop out in the wooden troughs, under the spiles. These troughs were hewed out of buckeye. This maple water was gathered up and put in a big kettle, hung on racks, with a big fire under it. It was then taken to the house and finished upon the stove. The skimmings after it got to the syrup stage was builed down and made into maple sugar for the children.

We wore tow linen clothes in summer and jeans in winter. Sister wore linsey in winter of different colors, dyed from herbs, especially poke berries; and wore unbleached cotton in summer, dyed with yellow mustard seed.

My grandfather, Jim Embry mended shoes and made fairly good ones.

There were four slaves. My mother did cooking and the men did the work. Bob Wheeler and Arch Bogie were our masters. Both were good and kind to us. I never saw a slave shipped, for my boss did not believe in that kind of punishment. My master had four boys, named Rube, Falton, Horace, and Billie. Rube and me played together and when we acted bad old Marse always licked Rube three or four times harder then he did me because Rube was older. Their daughter was named American Wheeler, for her mother.

White folks did not teach us to read and write. I learned that after I left my white folks. There was no church for slaves, but we went to the white folks church at Mr. Freedom. We sat in the gallery. The first colored preacher I ever heard was old man Leroy Estill. He preached in the Freedom meeting house (Baptist). I stood on the banks of Paint Lick Creek and saw my mother baptized, but do not remember the preachers name or any of the songs they sung.

We did not work on Saturday afternoon. The men would go fishing, and the women would go to the neighbors and help each other piece quilts. We used to have big times at the corn shuckings. The neighbors would come and help. We would have camp fires and sing songs, and usually a big dance at the barn when the corn was shucked. Some of the slaves from other plantations would pick the banjo, then the dance. Miss America married Sam Ward.

I was too young to remember only that they had good things to eat.

I can remember when my mothers brother died. He was buried at the Wheeler, but I do not recall any of the songs, and they did not have a preacher. My mother took his death so hard.

There was an old ash hopper, made of slats, put together at the bottom and wide at the top. The ashes were dumped in this and water poured over them. A drip was made and lye caught in wooden troughs. This was then boiled down and made into soap. My mother let me help stir it many a time. Then the big kettle would be lifted from the fire and left until cold. My mother would then block it off, and put on a wooden plank to dry out until ready for use."

Bibliography:
Interview with Dan Bogie, Ex-Slave.

GARRARD COUNTY. EX-SLAVE STORIES.
(ELIZA ISON) [HW: KY 13]
INTERVIEW WITH GEORGE HENDERSON:

GEORGE HENDERSON

Uncle George tells me that he was born May 10, 1860 near Versailles, in Woodford County, Kentucky. His father's name was Bradford Henderson, who was a slave of Milford Twiman who belonged to the Cleveland family. He does not know where his family came from. There were 21 children including two or three sets of twins. All died while young, except his brothers: Milford, Sam, and Joe; and sisters: Elle and Betsy. All the slaves lived in log cabins and there were about 30 or 40 of them on a plantation of 400 acres. "The cabin I was born in had four rooms, two above and two below. The rooms above were called lofts, and we climbed up a ladder to get to these rooms. We slept on trundle-beds, which were covered with straw ticks. Our covers were made in big patches from old cast-off clothes. When we got up in the morning we shoved the trundle bed back under the big bed. Some boy would ring a great big bell, called the "farm bell" about sunrise. Some went to the stables to look after the horses and mules. Plowing was done with a yoke or oxen. The horses were just used for carriages and to ride. My work was pulling weeds, feeding chickens, and helping to take care of the pigs. Marse Cleveland had a very bad male hog and had to keep him in a pen about 10 feet high. Sometimes he would break out of the pen and it would take all the bulldogs in the county to get him back. I never did earn any money, but worked for my food and clothes. My daddy used to hunt rabbits and possums. I went with him and would ride on his back with my feet in his pockets. He had a dog named Brutus which was a watch dog. My daddy would lay his hat down anywhere in the woods and Brutus would stay by the hat until he would come back. We ate all kinds of wild food, possum, and rabbits baked in a big oven. Minnows were fished from the creeks and fried in hot grease. We ate this with pone corn bread. We had plenty of vegetables to eat. An old negro called "Ole Man Ben" called us to eat. We called him the dinner bell because he would say "Who-e-e, God-dam your blood and guts".

Out clothes were made of jeens and linsey in winter. In the summer we wore cotton clothes. They gave us shoes at Christmas time. We were measured with sticks. Once I was warming my shoes on a back log on the big fire place, they fell over behind the logs and burnt up. I didn't marry while on the plantation.

My master and mistress lived in the big brick house of 15 rooms, with two long porches. One below and one below. My mistus was Miss Lucy Elmore before she married. Her children were named Miss Mat, Miss Emma, and Miss Jennie.

I saw the slaves in chains after they were sold. The white folks did not teach us to read and write. We had church on the plantation but we went from one plantation to another to hear preaching. White folks preacher's name was Reuben Lee, in Versailles. A meeting of the Baptist Church resulted in the first baptizing I ever saw. It was in Mr. Chillers pond. The preacher would say 'I am baptizing you in Mr. Chillers pond because I know he is an honest man'. I can't remember any funeral.

I remember one slave named Adams who ran away and when he came back my old master picked up a log from the fire and hit him over the head. We always washed up and cleaned up for Sunday. Some time the older ones would get drunk.

On Christmas and New Years day we would go up to the house and they would give us candy and fruit and fire-crackers. We were given some of all the food that the white folks had, even turkey. Would have heaps of corn-shuckings, the neighbors would come in and then we'd have big dances and old Marse would always have a "jug of licker".

If a cat crossed our path we would turn backwards for a while. When I was about 9 or 10 years old I went from the cabin to the big kitchen to make the fire for my mammy to get the breakfast and I saw ole man Billie Cleveland standing looking up in the sky. He had been dead about 3 or 4 years; but I saw him.

The white folks looked after us when we were sick. Used dock leaves, slippery elm for poultices. They put polk root in whiskey and gave it to us.

When the news came we were freed every body was glad. The slaves cleared up the ground and cut down trees. Stayed with Marse Cleveland the first year after the war. Have heard the Klu Klux Klan ride down the road, wearing masks. None ever bothered me or any of Marse Clevelands slaves.

I married years after I left Marse Cleveland. Married Lucy Mason the first time and had three children, two girls and 1 boy. I didn't have no children by my second marriage, but the third time I had four. One died. I have eight grandchildren.

We had no overseer but Marse Hock was the only boy and the oldest child. We had no white trash for neighbors. I have seen old covered wagons pulled by oxen travelling on the road going to Indianny and us children was whipped to keep us away from the road for fear they would steal us."

Bibliography:
Interview with George Henderson, Ex-slave.

GARRARD COUNTY. EX-SLAVE STORIES.
(ELIZA ISON) [HW: KY 11]
AUNT HARRIET MASON—EX-SLAVE:

HARRIET MASON

She was born one mile below Bryantsville on the Lexington Pike in Garrard County, and was owned by B.M. Jones. She gives the date of her birth as April 14, 1847. Aunt Harriet's father was Daniel Scott, a slave out of Mote Scott's slave family. Aunt Harriet's mother's name was Amy Jones, slave of Marse Briar Jones, who came from Harrodsburg, Ky. The names of her brothers were Harrison, Daniel, Merida, and Ned; her sisters were Susie and Maria. Miss Patsy, wife of Marse Briar gave Maria to Marse Sammy Welsh, brother of Miss Patsy's and who lived with his sister. He taught school in Bryantsville for a long time. "General Gano who married Jane Welsh, adopted daughter of Marse Briar Jones, took my sisters Myra and Emma, Brother Ned and myself to Tarrant County, Texas to a town called Lick Skillet, to live. Grapevine was the name of the white folks house. It was called Grapevine because these grapevines twined around the house and arbors. Sister Emma was the cook and Myra and me were nurse and house maids. Brother married Betty Estill, a slave who cooked for the Estill family. Mr. Estill later bought Ned in order to keep him on the place. I didn't sleep in the cabins with the rest of the Negroes; I slept in the big house and nursed the children. I was not paid any money for my work. My food was the same as what the white folks et. In the summer time we wore cotton and tow linen; and linsey in the winter. The white folks took me to church and dressed me well. I had good shoes and they took me to church on Sunday. My master was a preacher and a doctor and a fine man. Miss Mat sho was hard to beat. The house they lived in was a big white house with two long porches. We had no overseer or driver. We had no "Po white neighbors". There was about 300 acres of land around Lick Skillet, but we did not have many slaves. The slaves were waked up by General Gano who rang a big farm bell about four times in the morning. There was no jail on the place and I never say a slave whipped or punished in any way. I never saw a slave auctioned off. My Mistus taught all the slaves to read and write, and we set on a bench in the dining room. When the news came that we were free General Gano took us all in the dining room and told us about it. I told him I wusn't going to the cabins and sleep with them niggers and I didn't. At Christmas and New Years we sho did have big times and General Gano and Miss Nat would buy us candy, popcorn, and firecrackers and all the good things just like the white folks. I don't remember any weddings, but do remember the funeral of Mr. Marion who lived between the big house and Lick Skillet. He was going to be buried in the cemetery at Lick Skillet, but the horses got scared and turned the spring wagon over and the corpse fell out. The mourners sure had a time getting things straightened out, but they finally got him buried.

They used to keep watermelon to pass to company. Us children would go to the patch and bring the melons to the big spring and pour water over them and cool 'em. When news came that we were free we all started back to Kentucky to Marse Jones old place. We started the journey in two covered wagons and an ambulance. General Gano and Miss Nat and the two children and me rode in the ambulance. When we got to Memphis we got on a steam boat named "Old Kentucky". We loaded the ambulance and the two wagons and horses on the boat. When we left the boat, we got on the train and got off at Georgetown in Scott County and rode from there to General Gano's Brother William in Scott County, on a stage coach. When I took the children, Katy and Maurice, upstairs to wash them I looked out the window into the driveway and saw the horses that belonged to Marse Briar Jones. They nickered at the gate trying to get in. The horses were named Henry Clay and Dan. When the children went down I waved at the horses and they looked up at the window and nickered again and seemed to know me. When we were coming back from Texas, Maurice held on the plait of my hair all the way back. I didn't marry while I belonged to the Gano family. I married Henry Mason after I came to Lancaster to live about sixty years ago. I am the mother of nine children, three boys and six girls. There are two living. I have no grand-children. I joined the church when the cholera epidemic broke out in Lancaster in 1878. The preacher was Brother Silas Crawford, of the Methodist Church. I was baptized in a pond on Creamery Street. I think people ought to be religious because they live better and they love people more."

Aunt Harriet lived at the present behind the White Methodist Church in Lancaster. The daughter with whom she lives is considered one of the high class of colored people in Lancaster. She holds an A.B. Degree, teaching in the colored city school, and is also a music teacher. She stands by the teaching of her mother, being a "Good Methodist"; giving of her time, talent, and service for her church.

Bibliography:
Interview with Aunt Harriet Mason, Lancaster, Kentucky.

GARRARD COUNTY. EX-SLAVE STORIES.
(ELIZA ISON)

INTERVIEW WITH BERT MAYFIELD:

BERT MAYFIELD

Bert Mayfield was born in Garrard County, May 29, 1852, two miles south of Bryantsville on Smith Stone's place. His father and mother were Ped and Matilda Stone Mayfield, who were slaves of Smith Stone who came from Virginia. His brothers were John, Harrison, Jerry, and Laurence, who died at an early age.

He lived on a large plantation with a large old farm house, built of logs and weatherboards, painted white. There were four rooms on the first floor, and there were also finished rooms on the second floor. An attic contained most of the clothes needed for the slaves. "Uncle Bert" in his own language says, "On Christmas each of us stood in line to get our clothes; we were measured with a string which was made by a cobbler. The material had been woben by the slaves in a plantation shop. The flax and hemp were raised on the plantation. The younger slaves had to "swingle it" with a wooden instrument, somewhat like a sword, about two feet long, and called a swingler. The hemp was hackled by the older slaves. The hackle was an instrument made of iron teeth, about four inches long, one-half inch apart and set in a wooden plank one and one-half feet long, which was set on a heavy bench. The hemp stalks were laid on these benches and hackled herds were then pulled through and heaped in piles and taken to the work shops where it was twisted and tied then woven, according to the needs. Ropes, carpets, and clothing were made from this fiber.

"Our cabins were usually one room with a loft above which we reached by a ladder. Our beds were trundle beds with wheels on them to push them under the big beds. We slept on straw ticks covered with Lindsey quilts, which were made from the cast-off clothes, cut into squares and strips."

Bert can just remember his grandparents.

He would feed pigs; pulled "pusley" out of the garden for them "and them pigs loved it mighty well".

No money was paid for work. Bacon and "pone bread" baked in the yard in an oven that had legs and lid on top was the chief food and his favorite. The coals were put on top as well as under the oven. They drank sweet milk and butter milk, but no coffee; they also ate cabbage, squash, sweet and Irish potatoes, which were cooked with, skins on, greased, and put in the oven. "Possum" and coon hunts were big events, they would hunt all night. The possums were baked in the ovens and usually with sweet potatoes in their mouths. The little boys would fish, bringing home their fish to be scaled by rubbing them between their hands, rolled in meal and cooked in a big skillet. "We would eat these fish with pone corn bread and we sho' had big eatins!"

Marse Stone had a big sugar camp with 300 trees. We would be waked up at sun-up by a big horn and called to get our buckets and go to the sugar camps and bring water from the maple trees. These trees had been tapped and elderwood spiles were placed in the taps where the water dripped to the wooden troughs below. We carried this water to the big poplar troughs which were about 10 feet long and 3 feet high. The water was then dipped out and placed in different kettles to boil until it became the desired thickness for "Tree Molasses". Old Miss Polly would always take out enough of the water to boil down to make sugar cakes for us boys. We had great times at these "stirrin' offs" which usually took place at night.

The neighbors would usually come and bring their slaves. We played Sheep-meat and other games. Sheep-meat was a game played with a yarn ball and when one of the players was hit by the ball that counted him out. One song we would always sing was "Who ting-a-long? Who ting-a-long? Who's been here since I've been gone? A pretty girl with a josey on".

There was no slave jail on the Stone place, and I never saw a slave sold or auctioned off. I was told that one of our slaves ran off and was gone for three years. Some white person wrote him to come home that he was free. He was making his own way in Ohio and stopped in Lexington, Kentucky for breakfast; while there he was asked to show his Pass papers which he did, but they were forged so he was arrested. Investigators soon found that his owner was Mr. Stone who did not wish to sell him and sent for him to come home. Uncle Ned's own Tim said he "would go fetch him back" but instead he sold him to a southern slave trader. My old Mistus Meg taught me how to read from an old national spelling book, but I did not learn to write. We had no church, but the Bible was read to us on Sunday afternoons by some of the white folks. The first Church I remember was the Old Fork Baptist Church about four miles from Lancaster on the Lexington Pike. The first preacher I remember was Burdette Kemper. I heard him preach at the old church where my Mistus and Master took me every Sunday. The first Baptizin' that I remember was on Dix Fiver near Floyd's Mill. Preacher Kemper did the Baptizin' and Ellen Stone, one of our slaves was Baptized there with a number of others—whites and blacks too. When Ellen came up out of the water she was clapping her hands and shouting. One of the songs I remember at this Baptizing was:

> "Come sinners and Saints and hear me tell
>   The wonders of E-Man-u-el,
> Who brought my soul with him to dwell
>   And give me heavenly union."

"The first funeral sermon I remember was preached by John Moran, negro at the first Baptist here in Lancaster.

"The negroes would talk among themselves, but never carried tales to the white folks. I never heard of any trouble between blacks and whites. On Sunday's we would hold prayer meetings among ourselves. The neighbors would come when slaves were sick. Old Mistus looked after us, giving us teas made of catnip and vermifuge. Poultices of dock leaves and slippery elm were also used when were sick. Some of the slaves wore rabbit feet for charms and skins of snakes for a belt as a charm.

"My first wedding was 53 years ago. The woman was named Emma Barren, raised by Dr. Pettus. I had no children. We went to Mr. Spencer Hubble to live, in Lincoln County. We had no chil [TR: This sentence appears to have been unfinished or erased.]

I received the first news of freedom joyfully. I went to old man Onstott's to live. I lived there two or three years. I think Abe Lincoln a great man. He did not believe in slavery and would have paid the southern people for their slaves if he had lived. All the slaves on Morse Stone's place were treated well.

Bibliography:
Interview with Bert Mayfield.

United States. Work Projects Administration

MERCER COUNTY. EX-SLAVE STORIES.
(HAZEL CINNAMON)

INTERVIEW WITH WILL OATS—EX-SLAVE:

WILL OATS

Will Oats, 84 years of age, was born in Wayne County, up Spring Valley in 1854. He was the son of Betty Oats and Will Garddard of North Carolina. He has three sisters: Lucy Wilson, Frances Phillips that live in Ohio, and Alice Branton of Mercer County, Kentucky. He has two brothers; Jim Coffey and Lige Coffey of Harrodsburg.

As a child he lived with his mother, brothers, sisters, and grandmother. Their quarters were in the yard of their master; and they were as comfortable as any slaves—with plenty to eat and clothes to keep them warm.

Will was just a boy at that time, and he cut wood and carried it in; and did other chores around the house such as help to milk and feed the stock. Their food was plentiful and they ate all kinds of vegetables, and had plenty of milk and butter, fat meat, and bread.

The family all wore home made clothing, cotton shirts, heavy shoes, very heavy underwear; and if they wore out their winter shoes before the spring weather they had to do without until the fall.

Will was owned by Lewis Oats and his sister; they lived in a two story house, built of log and weather boarded. They were very wealthy people. The farm consisted of over 230 acres; they owned six slaves; and they had to be up doing their morning work before the master would wake.

When working and the slaves would disobey their master, they were punished in some way; but there was no jail. They didn't know how to read or write, and they had no church to attend. All they had to do when not at work was to talk to the older folks. On Christmas morning they would usually have a little extra to eat and maybe a stick of candy. On New Year's Day their work went on just the same as on any other day.

Will, as a boy loved to play marbles which was about the most interesting game they had to play. Of course, they could play outside as all children do now when they had spare time.

At that time there were few doctors and when the slaves would get hurt or sick, they were usually looked after by the master or by their overseer.

After the war had closed, Will's grandmother walked from Monticello to Camp Nelson to get her free papers and her children. They were all very happy, but they were wondering what they were going to do without a home, work, or money. But after Will and his mother and grandmother got their freedom, the grandmother bought a little land and house and they all went there to live. Of course, they worked out for other people and raised a great deal of what they ate. Will lived there until he grew older and went out for himself; and later moved to Mercer County where he now lives.

Bibliography:
Interview with Will Oats, Ex-Slave of Mercer County.

United States. Work Projects Administration

GARRARD COUNTY. EX-SLAVE STORIES.
(ELIZA ISON)

AUNT BELLE ROBINSON:

BELLE ROBINSON

I found Aunt Belle sitting on the porch, dressed nice and clean with a white handkerchief pinned on her neck. When I went to her and told her who I was and the reason for my visit her face beamed with smiles and she said "Lawdy, it has been so long that I have forgot nearly everything I knew".

Further investigation soon proved that she had not forgotten, for her statements were very intelligent. She was working on a quilt and close investigation found that the work was well done. Aunt Belle tells me "I was born June 3rd, 1853 in Garrard County near Lancaster. My mother's name was Marion Blevin and she belonged to the family of Pleas Blevin. My father's name was Arch Robinson who lived in Madison County. Harrison Brady bought me from Ole Miss Nancy Graham and when Mr. Brady died and his property was sold Mrs. Brady bought me back; and she always said that she paid $400 for me. I lived in that family for three generations, until every one of them died. I was the only child and had always lived at the big house with my mistus. I wore the same kind of clothes and ate the same kind of food the white people ate. My mother and father lived at the cabin in the yard and my mother did the cooking for the family. My father did the work on the farm with the help that was hired from the neighbors. I was too young to remember much about the slave days, but I never heard of any slaves of the neighbors being punished. My "Mistus" always took me to the Baptist Church with her. I do not remember any preacher's names or any songs they sang."

Bibliography:
 Interview with Aunt Belle Robinson, Ex-Slave of Garrard County.

MONROE COUNTY. FOLKLORE.
(LENNETH JONES-242) [HW: ESSAY]

UNCLE EDD SHIRLEY (97):
JANITOR AT TOMPKINSVILLE DRUG CO. AND HOSPITAL, TOMPKINSVILLE, KY.

EDD SHIRLEY

I am 97 years old and am still working as janitor and support my family. My father was a white man and my mother was a colored lady. I was owned three different times, or rather was sold to three different families. I was first owned by the Waldens; then I was sold to a man by the name of Jackson, of Glasgow, Kentucky. Then my father, of this county, bought me.

I have had many slave experiences. Some slaves were treated good, and some were treated awful bad by the white people; but most of them were treated good if they would do what their master told them to do.

I onced saw a light colored gal tied to the rafters of a barn, and her master whipped her until blood ran down her back and made a large pool on the ground. And I have seen negro men tied to stakes drove in the ground and whipped because they would not mind their master; but most white folks were better to their slaves and treated them better than they are now. After their work in the fields was finished on Saturday, they would have parties and have a good time. Some old negro man would play the banjo while the young darkies would dance and sing. The white folks would set around and watch; and would sometimes join in and dance and sing.

My colored grand father lived to be 115 years old, and at that age he was never sick in his life. One day he picked up the water bucket to go to the spring, and as he was on his way back he dropped dead.

GARRARD COUNTY. EX-SLAVE STORIES.
(ELIZA ISON)

INTERVIEW WITH EX-SLAVE UNCLE WES WOODS:

WES WOODS

My first visit to uncle Wes Wood, and his wife Aunt Lizzie Wood, found them in their own comfortable little home in Duncantown, a nice urban section of the town, where most of the inhabitants are of the better class of colored people. A small yard with a picket fence and gate surround the yard, which had tall hollyhocks, rearing their heads high above the fence.

A knock on the front door brought the cordial invitation "to come in". Upon entering, I was invited to have a chair and "rest my hat". After seating myself and making inquiry as to their health, I told them the object of my visit, and their faces beamed when I asked if they remembered "slave days". Aunt Lizzie set down the can of beans she was preparing for their meal and said with a clasp of her hands, "Lawsey, Honey, what I do know would fill a book".

Uncle Wes had been a "shut-in" for eleven months, and was in bed, but was cheerful and bright with an intelligent memory, rarely found in one his age. Uncle Wes tells me that he was born May 21, 1864 in Garrard County, near Cartersville, and was first a slave of Mrs. Eliza Kennedy, who later married John Yeakey, of that section of the county. "My father's name was Ben Woods, my mother's name was Janie Woods, but I do not know what family she belonged to except the Woods. My master owned about three or four hundred acres of land, and there were about twenty slaves, including the children.

There were three or four cabins for the slaves to live in, not so very far from the house. The cabin where my mother and father lived was the closest to the house, for my mother did the cooking. Our cabin was one long room, with a loft above, which we reached with a ladder. There was one big bed, with a trundle bed, which was on wooden rollers and was shoved under the big bed in the daytime. The oldest boys slept in a big wooden bed in the loft. The cabins were built of logs and chinked with rock and mud. The ceiling was of joists, and my mother used to hang the seed that we gathered in the fall, to dry from these joists. Some of the chimneys were made with sticks and chinked with mud, and would sometimes catch on fire. Later people learned to build chimneys of rock with big wide fire places, and a hearth of stone, which made them safer from fire.

Second Interview:

"I chopped corn and pulled weeds and the other work hands would let me ride behind them beck to the big house, and My! how hungry I wuz and how we did eat. We would have beans, cooked in a big kettle in the back yard, cabbage and potatoes, with corn pone bread, baked in a big oven In the yard and plenty of good buttermilk to drink.

"My young bosses, when I lived in the Kennedy family would take the dogs and let me go coon hunting at night with them, and what big times we had. The possums were skinned and cooked in a big kettle hung over the fire, then taken out and put in a big oven to take. A piece of streaked meat was put in and a small pod of red pepper—My-My what eatin' we had!

"We fished with a stock pole and a twine string. We had big times hunting fishing worms for bait. We used to catch Hockney, Hads and Chubs. My mistus would not let me go fishing on Sunday, but I would slip off and go anyhow. I nearly always had a good string caught and I would tie them to a branch on the creek until the next day; then I would go fishing and in about two hours I would come back with the fish, and she would say, "Wes, you had good luck today"; and I would say, "Yes Mistus, I did", but never did I tell her when I caught the fish.

"My first wife was Lou Burnsides and we had five children: Eliza, Fannie, George, Julia, and Jennie. All of them are dead but two. I have no children by my present wife.

"I never saw a slave whipped or in chains. My boss did not believe in that kind of punishment. If the children needed whipping, it was done like all other children are whipped when they need it.

"The first colored preacher I recall was named John Reed, a Baptist preacher at Paint Lick. I joined the church at Lowell, not very far from here. The preachers name was Leroy Estill, a "Predestinerian".

"Marse Woods had five children, two boys and three girls, none of them are living.

"We were glad when the news came that we were free, but none of us left for a long time, not until the Woods family was broken up. My father hired me out to work for my vituals and clothes, and I got $25.00 at the end of the year. I do not remember of any wedding or death in my old masters house.

"I believe in heart-felt religion and prayer. The Good Book teaches us we must be prepared for another world after this. I want to go to Heaven when I die, and I try to live by the Bible."

Bibliography:
Interview with Wes Woods, Ex-Slave of Garrard County.

COMBINED INTERVIEWS:
CUSTOMS: BY COUNTIES
SLAVERY: LOCAL HISTORY AND DIALECT
ANDERSON CO.
(Mildred Roberts)

Story of Ann Gudgel (age unknown):

ANN GUDGEL

"I doesn't know how old I am, but I was a little girl when dat man Lincum freed us niggahs. My mammy neber tole us our age, but I knows I'se plenty old, cause I feels like it.

"When I was a liddle girl all of us was owned by Master Ball. When Lincum freed us neggahs, we went on and libbed with Master Ball till us chilluns was bout growed up. None of us was eber sold, cause we belonged to the Balls for always back as far as we could think.

"Mammy worked up at the big house, but us chilluns had to stay at de cabin. But I didn't berry much care, cause ole Miss had a liddle child jest bout my age, and us played together.

"The onliest time ole Miss eber beat me was when I caused Miss Nancy to get et up wit de bees. I tole her

'Miss Nancy, de bees am sleep, lets steal de honey.' Soon as she tetched it, day flew all ober us, and it took Mammy bout a day to get the stingers outen our haids. Ole Miss jest natually beat me up bout dat.

"One day they vaccinated all de slaves but mine neber took atall. I nebber tole noboddy, but I jest set right down by de fireplace and rubbed wood ashes and juice that spewed outen de wood real hard ober de scratch. All de others was real sick and had the awfullest arms, but mine neber did eben hurt."

UNION CO.
(RUBY GARTEN)

MRS. HEYBURN:

MRS. HEYBURN

(These two stories were told by Mrs. Heyburn as she remembered them from her grandmother).

"When the War was going on between the States and the Confederate soldiers had gone south, the Yankee soldiers came through. There was a little negro slave boy living on the farm and he had heard quite a bit about the Yankees, so one day they happened to pass through where he could see them and he rushed into the house and said, "Miss Lulu, I saw a Yankee, and he was a man."

"I remember the slaves on my grandfather's farm. After they were freed they asked him to keep them because they didn't want to leave. He told them they could stay and one of the daughters of the slaves was married in the kitchen of my grandfather's house. After the wedding they set supper for them. Some of the slave owners were very good to their slaves; but some whipped them until they made gashes in their backs and would put salt in the gashes.

CALLOWAY CO.
(L. CHERRY)

STORY OF UNCLE GEORGE SCRUGGS, A COLORED SLAVE:

GEORGE SCRUGGS

I wuz a slave befo de wa. My boss, de man dat I b'long to, wuz Ole Man Vol Scruggs. He wuz a race hoss man. He had a colod boy faw evy hoss dem days and a white man faw evy hoss, too. I wuz bawn rite here in Murry. My boss carrid me away frum here. I thought a heap uv him and he though a heap uv me. I'd rub de legs uv dem hosses and rode dem round to gib em excise. I wuz jes a small boy when my boss carrid me away from Murry. My boss carrid me to Lexinton. I staid wid Ole Man Scruggs a long time. I jes don no how long. My boss carrid me to his brother, Ole Man Finch Scruggs. He run a sto and I had to sweep de flo uv de sto, wash dishes and clean nives and falks evy day. Ole Man Finch Scruggs carrid my uncle up thar wen Ole Vol carrid me. Ole Man Finch Scruggs liv'd at a little town called Clintinvil on tuther side uv Lexinton. Wen Ole man Vol Scruggs marid, he take me away from Old Man Finch Scruggs and carrid me to liv wid him. I wuz den wid my ole boss again. He den hired me to wuk faw a docta in Lexinton. My job wuz to clean up his ofis and wen he went out en de cuntry, he took me long to open de gates. I had to skowa nives and fawks and ole brass canel stix. Dats been a long time ago, Ize tellin you, white man. While I wuz sweepin de doctas ofis one day I saw droves uv colud folks gwine by wid two white men ridin in front, two ridin in de midel, and two ridin behind. De colud folks wuz wulkin, gwine down town to be sold. When I fust seen em comin I got scared an started to run but de white man said, "stop, boy, we is not gwine a hurt you." I staid wid dat boss docta sumpin like a yer, an den wont back to my Ole Boss. I'd a been up thar wid im yet but he kep telin me I wuz free. But I diden no whut he mean by sich talk. Wen my Ole Boss sole out up thar, he brung me wid him on to Paducah.

He had a neffu in de wholesale grocy bisness in Paducah. My Old Boss carrid me to his neffu and lef me thar. Dat wuz de las time I eva saw my good Ole Boss caus he went on to Missouri. My Old Boss wuz sho good to me, white man. I sho do luv im yet. Wy, he neva wood low me to go barfooted, caus he wuz afraid I'd stick thorns in my feet, an if he eva caut me barfooted, he sho wod make my back tell it. Wen he lef me in Paducah, his neffu took me over to my ant, Rose Scruggs to stay all nite wid her. Nex day I walked wid my cousin to Mayfield, carryin two toe sacks uv cloes dat my Good Ole Boss give me wen he lef me in Paducah. De cloze wuz faw me an my muther. Wen we got to Mayfield, we went strate to Judge Williams caus he marrid my Ole Boss' sister and I wuz sho we could stay wid dem. My Ole Boss an my muther wuz play-children together. My muther's name wuz Patsy Malone. Mr. Maline's wife wuz my Ole Boss' sister and my muther fell to her as a slave. Next day I come to Murry whar my muther lived wid Miss Emily Malone. I wuz gone a long time caus my Ole Boss took me way from Murry wen I wuz a small boy. I staid wid my muther til she died. I now live in one mile uv de house whar I wuz bawn. Mr. Hugh Wear sez I is 100 years old.

United States. Work Projects Administration

GARRARD CO.
(SUE HIGGINS)

STORY OF AUNT HARRIET MASON AGE 100—A SLAVE GIRL:

HARRIET MASON

"When I was seven years old my missis took me to Bourbon County, when we got to Lexington I tried to run off and go back to Bryantsville to see my mammy. Mas'r Gano told me if I didn't come the sheriff would git me. I never liked to go to Lexington since.

"One Sunday we was going to a big meetin' we heared som'in rattling in the weeds. It was a big snake, it made a track in the dust. When we got home missis asked me if I killed any snakes. I said to missis, snake like to got me and Gilbert, too.

"They used to have dances at Mrs. Dickerson's, a neighbor of General Gano (a preacher in the Christian Church). Mrs. Dickerson wouldn't let the "Padaroes" come to the dances. If they did come, whe[TR:she?] would get her pistol and make them leave.

"When General Gano went from Texas to Kentucky, he

brought 650 head of horses. He sold all of them but Old Black.

"Mas'r Gano went back to Texas to take up a child he had buried there. The boat blowed up, and he came nigh gittin' drowned.

"One time I wus out in Mas'rs wheat field. I would get the wheat heads and make chewin' wax. I told missis I want to go up to Bryantsville to see my mammy. Mas'r took me in about a week.

"Up at Miss Jennie West's house they had an ole icehouse. Some boys made out like they had a bear up there to scare every body away.

"I saw a flock of wild geese fly over one evenin' late. Some boys saw them and one boy shot the leader. The rest of the flock wound round and round, they didn't know where to go.

"One time when I was actin' nurse for missis, there was another nigger gal there and we was playin' horse-shoes. Celia hit me in the head. It got blood all over the baby's dress. Missis came out, she say, "I'll hit you niggers if you don't stop playing with horse-shoes." The scar is on my head yet whar Celia hit me. I ain't played since. Do you blame me?

"Missis told her brother Sam one day to whoop me. Every time he hit me, I'd hit him. I wan't feared then. I didn't know no better. Look like white folks goin' to have their way and niggers goin' to have theirs.

"I used to say I wish I'd died when I was little. But now I

thank De Lord I'm here and I want to stay here as long as Lilly (my daughter) lives.

"Missis wanted all of us little niggers to call Kate, Missis' little daughter, Miss Kate. But missis say, "They will call me old missis then".

"Kate had red hair. A little nigger boy say, 'Look! Harriet, the town's on fire', I say git away from here nigger, I ain't goin' to have you makin' fun of my chil'en.

"Me and missis was goin' to a neighbor's house one day in a sleigh. The baby was wrapped up in a comfort (it had a hole in it). The baby slipped out. I say, 'Lor' missis, you're lost that baby.'

"No, I haven't, Missis say. We stopped and shook the comfort and John was gone. 'Ain't that awful, Miss Mat?' We went back and found him a mile behind."

I asked Aunt Harriet to sing. She said, "I have to wait for the speret to move me". (S. Higgins).

United States. Work Projects Administration

BOYD CO.
(CARL F. HALL)

REV. JOHN R. COX:

REV. JOHN R. COX

It is probable that slave labor was more expensive to the white masters than free labor would have been. Beside having cost quite a sum a two-year old negro child brought about $1,500 in the slave market, an adult negro, sound and strong, cost from $5,000 up to as high as $25,000, or more. The master had to furnish the servant his living. The free employee is paid only while working; when sick, disabled or when too old to work, his employer is no longer responsible.

A slave owner, in West Virginia, bought a thirteen year old black girl at an auction. When this girl was taken to his home she escaped, and after searching every where, without finding her, he decided that she had been helped to escape and gave her up as lost. About two years after that a neighbor, on a closely farm, was in the woods feeding his cattle, he saw what he first thought was a bear, running into the thicket from among his cows. Getting help, he rounded up the cattle and searching the thick woodland, finally found that what he had supposed was a wild animal, was the long lost fugitive black girl. She had lived all this time in caves, feeding on nuts, berries, wild apples and milk from cows, that she could catch and milk. Returned to her master she was sold to a Mr. Morgan Whittaker who lived near where Prestonsburg, Kentucky now is.

A Dr. David Cox, physician from Scott County, Virginia, who treated Mr. Whitaker for a cancer, saw this slave girl, who had become a strong healthy young woman, and Mr. Whitaker unable to otherwise pay his doctor bill, let Dr. Davis have her for the debt.

At this time the slave girl was about twenty-one years of age, and Dr. Davis took her home to Scott County, Virginia where he married her to his only other slave, George Cox, by the ceremony of laying a broom on the floor and having the two young negroes step over the broom stick.

Among the children of George Cox and his wife was Rev. John R. Cox, Col. who now lives in Catlettsburg, Kentucky, and is probably the only living ex-slave in this county.

After the Emancipation Proclamation, by President Lincoln, in 1865, John managed to get four years of schooling where he learned to read and write and become very proficient in arithmetic.

He says that had he had the opportunity to study that we have today he could have been the smartest man in the United States. He also says, that before freedom, the negroes in his neighborhood were allowed no books, if found looking at a book a slave was whipped unmercifully.

John's master, in allowing his slaves to marry, was much

more liberal than most other slave owners, who allowed their slaves no such liberty.

As a rule negro men were not allowed to marry at all, any attempt to mate with the negro women brought swift, sure horrible punishment and the species were propogated by selected male negroes, who were kept for that purpose, the owners of this privileged negro, charged a fee of one out of every four of his offspring for his services.

The employing class of Kentuckians, many of them descendants of slave owners, are prone to be reactionary in their attitude towards those who toil, this is reflected in low wages and inferior working conditions, a condition which affects both white and black labor alike, in many sections of the state. (Bibliography: Rev. John R. Cox (colored) Catlettsburg, Kentucky. Born 1852 (does not know day and month), Minister A.M.E. Church. First truant officer Catlettsburg, Kentucky. Interviewed Dec. 23, 1936.)

United States. Work Projects Administration

WAYNE CO.
(GERTRUDE VOGLER)

[MRS. DUNCAN:]

MRS. DUNCAN

"After the War was over mammie's old man did not want us with them, so he threatened to kill us. Then my old mammie fixed us a little bundle of what few clothes we had and started us two children out to go back to the Campbell family in Albany. The road was just a wilderness and full of wild animals and varmints. Mammie gave us some powder and some matches, telling us to put a little down in the road every little while and set fire to it. This would scare the wild animals away from us.

"We got to the river at almost dark and some old woman set us across the river in a canoe. She let us stay all night wit her, and we went on to 'Grandpap Campbells'' (We always called him grandpap instead of master, as the others did.) When he saw us comin' he said 'Lawd have mercy here comes them poor little chillun'.

"I stayed with them that time until I was big enough to be a house girl. Then I went to live with the Harrison family in Albany; and I lived with them till I married old Sam

Duncan and come to Wayne County to live. I've raised a family of nine children and have thirty-seven grand children and twenty great grand children.

"Every one of my children wears a silver dime on a string around their leg, to keep off the witches spell. One time, before my daughter Della got to wearing it, she was going down the road, not far from our house, when all at once her leg gave way and she could not walk. Of course I knowed what it was. So I went after Linda Woods, the witch doctor. She come with a bottle of something, all striped with all colors, but when you shake it up it was all the same color. She rubbed her leg with it and told me to get all the life everlasting (a weed you know) that I could carry in my arm, and brew it for tea to bathe her leg in. Then pour it in a hole in the ground, but not to cover it up. Then not to go down the same road for nine days.

"We did all she said, and her leg got all right as soon as we bathed it. But she did not wait nine days, and started down the road the next day. The very same thing happened to her again. Her leg give way under her and she could not walk a step.

"I went after Linda Woods again. This time she said, 'D—m her, I told her not to go over that road for nine days.' But she came with the striped bottle and destroyed the witch spell again, telling her this time if she went over the road again for nine days that she would remain a cripple all her life, for she would not cure her again.

"Della stayed off that road for nine days, this time, and all the family have worn the silver dime around their legs ever since.

"Another time my old man Sam got down in his back. Well, he went to Henry Coulter (he was another witch doctor). He just shot in the back with a glass pistol, and cured him. Of course there was not any bullet in the pistol, but it cured him. He could draw a picture of a chicken on a paper and shoot it, and a chicken would fall dead in the yard, yes sir. I've seen him do it. Old Henry is dead now though. When he died he had a whole trunk full of the queerest looking things you ever seed. And they took it all and buried it. Nobody would touch it for anything.

"I always keep a horse shoe over my door to keep the spirits away. We live very close to the graveyard, and my boy Ed said he had been seeing his brother Charley in his room every night. If he was livin' right he would not be seeing Charlie every night. Charlie never bothers me. He was my boy that died and is buried in this graveyard above our house."

United States. Work Projects Administration

DAVIES CO.
(CECELIA LASWELL)

[MRS. ELIZABETH ALEXANDER:]

MRS. ELIZABETH ALEXANDER

The following is a very old Negro sermon I found in an old scrap book dated 1839, belonging to Mrs. Elizabeth Alexander, Frederica St. She says she has heard her family refer to parts of it at different time in her early life and supposed that the negro preacher belonged to her people. Quote: Mine deerly fren: Ub dar's wun ting wot de Lord abominerates worser nor anudder; it is a wicked nigger! A wicked wite man's bad snuff, dur Lord nose! but dey so dam wite, an so kussed sarcy, day doun no no better, so dar's some appolleragee fur 'em; but I gin yer for th noe as how, a wicked nigger can nibber scape frum de vengence ob de Lord-day's no use playin possum any more dan day was ob Joner coorin it into de wale's belly! (Glory from the congregation) Let um go to de Norf Pole, or to de Souf Pole, to de West Pole, or to de East Pole, or de Poles in any ob de words; he ant a bit safer den he would be in a cellar at 5 pints, wid ole Hays arter him! (groans) Oh! niggers! I tink I see you look round. Yer's better! Fer wot I tells yer's trufe! Gorda mity's trufe! Werrily I say unter yer! Wen de court ob seshions ob de las day cum, ye'll reckerlect wot I say at dis times! Wen yer hab de Lord fer Recorder, an a jury ob angles, an Gabriel ter report der trial fer de hebbenly "Herald" (deep groans) Yas! den yar'll turn up de wite ob yer eyes! (Sighs) den ter'll call fer de rock ter cubber yer! An de hill ter fall top o' yer. No yer don't. Kase, in de fus place day woodn't do it; an in de libenth place, ub day would it would be no better dan ridin in a cart in de big city or gettin under de butcher's stall in de fly market; fer de Lord can move more mountins in wun minite, dan de biggest nigger in dis congregation could shake a stick at twixt now an next fort ob July (clapping of hands, sighs, groans and grunts) Tink, yer black sinners ob de bottomless pit, deeper dan de hole Holt bored fer water. Oh! yer'll wish yo cood bore fer wat-r dar! but day's no water dar, an de deeper yer go, Oh, my bredren, de deeper it git! An den de smell! Yer'll gib yer soul uv yer had any left, jist fur wun smell ob a rotten egg! Oh, my deelee frens some ob yer hold yer nose wen yer go by de gas works. How der yer spose yer'l feel dare yer smell notin but brimstone an nashin ob teeth! (deep groans) Oh, I hear yer groans, but I ant begin to cum ter worst yit. Oh! my toenail a'most shake off in ma stockin wen I tink ob dat heat ob infernal regins! Den yer tink melted led cold as de young gemmen at de big houses tink a miny julip is now, an besid's my brederen it keeps a burnin nite on day to de end ob ebrerlastin; yer needn't tink bimeby yer go from dare to hebben like de Rummin Catlick—No, in de fust place yer don't; an in de second if yer cood, yer'd git yer def of cole goin frum one place to tudder. An now, my belobbed brederen, lets in terwestigate how tar git bale;

how to avoid de Sing Sing ob de world wot's got to cume. Fiddlin an dancin wont do it. Yer'll neber git ter hebben by loafin, pitchin cents, an dancin Juba! De only way is ter support de preacher, gib yer money ter me, and I'll take yer sins on my shoulder. An now I beseech yer not ter leebe dis here holy place an go round er corner, round er corner and fergit de words yer have heered dis night. Next Wednesday ebenin dar will be a sarbice in his place de Lord willin, but next Thursday ebenin weffer or no. An now we will sing inti de 40-elebent him de particlarest meter.

> Old Ebe he was de second man fur Adam was de fust——
> A black man's made ob ebony, a white man's made o' dust.
>
> Methuselah was the oldest man, but Sampson was the strongest——
> Cats, rats, and puppies all hab tails, but monkies is der longest.

(While they were singing the 11th verse, I took my departure.—B.L.)

United States. Work Projects Administration

LAUREL CO.
(PERRY LARKEY)

AMELIA JONES:

AMELIA JONES

Concerning slaves of this section of the country, I will quote experiences and observation of an old negro lady who was a slave, Mrs. Amelia Jones, living in North London, Kentucky. "Aunt Amelia" as she is known around here is eighty-eight years of age, being sixteen years of age at the close of the Civil War.

Mrs. Jones says, "I will tell as best I can remember, I was born eighty-eight years ago in Manchester, Ky. under a master by the name of Daw White. he was southern republican and was elected as congressman by that party from Manchester, Ky. He was the son of Hugh White, the original founder of Whitesberg, Ky. Master White was good to the slaves, he fed us well and had good places for us to sleep, and didn't whip us only when it was necessary, but didn't hesitate to sell any of his slaves, he said, "You all belong to me and if you don't like it, I'll put you in my pocket" meaning of course that he would sell that slave and put the money in his pocket.

The day he was to sell the children from their mother he would tell that mother to go to some other place to do some work and in her absence he would sell the children. It was the same when he would sell a man's wife, he also sent him to another job and when he returned his wife would be gone. The master only said "don't worry you can get another one".

Mrs. Jones has a sister ninety-two years of age living with her now, who was sold from the auction block in Manchester. Her sister was only twelve years of age when sold and her master received $1,220.00 for her, then she was taken south to some plantation. Also her father was sold at that place at an auction of slaves at a high price, handcuffed and taken south. She never saw her father again. She says the day her father was sold there was a long line of slaves to be sold and after they were sold and a good price paid for each they were handcuffed and marched away to the South, her father was among the number.

The Auction block at Manchester was built in the open, from rough-made lumber, a few steps, and a platform on top of that, the slave to be sold. He would look at the crowd as the auctioneer would give a general description of the ability and physical standing of the man. He heard the bids as they came in wondering what his master would be like.

Mrs. Jones claims she had no privileges, but had as before stated plenty to eat and wear, and a good place to sleep; but most masters treated them cruel and beat them most of the time. They were also underfed at most places, but since they had such a good master they did not want for a thing.

Cemetery Hill as it is known to us here, being in London, Ky. was a hill on which a Civil War battle was fought. The trenches are still here. The hill was given to the north to bury their dead by Jarvis Jackson, a great grand father of the Jarvis Jackson who is now city police of London, today. By some reason, the soldiers were taken up and moved to a different place only a few years ago. Mrs. Hoage says "the first daisies that were brought to this contry were put on that hill" and she can remember when the entire hill was covered with them.

The southern side had trenches on the east side of the Dixie Highway on and surrounding the site where the Pennington Hospital is now standing, which are very vivid today. The London City School being in the path bears a hole today from a cannon ball. Shot no doubt from the Southern forces. The new addition to the school hides the hole, but until recent years it could be seen being about ten inches in diameter.

Zollie Coffer a southern general had camped at Wild Cat, Ky. but was forced to retreat when general Garrad and Lucas and Stratton two captains under him, all from Clay county, with a large crowd came in. He, on his retreat came through London and had a battle with an army of Ohioians camped on Cemetery Hill. Quoted a poem by Mrs. Hodge, which she remembered from those days:

> "Just raise your eyes to yon grassy hill,
> View the bold Ohioians working with skill,
> Their bombs lying around them to spew fiery flames,
> Among the seceders, till they wont own their names."

Mrs. Hodge quotes another poem from memory about Gen. Coffer's retreat from Wild Cat:

"Our tigers and bullpups to Wild Cat did go,
To fight our brave boys, tho our force they did not know.
When they come in gun shot distance, Schelf told them to halt,
We're not Murphey's honey, nor Alex Whites salt.

His orders to his men, was "go thru" or "go to hell"
But our Indiana hoosier bous, heard them too well,
In less than thirty minutes, they gave them many balls,
Wild Cat had had kittens, Oh; don't you hear them squall.

They did not stay long, before they did retreat,
Went on double quick and left all their meat,
As they went back through Barbourville, they say Zollie did say
I've lost fifteen hundred killed or run away.

Away back in Mississippi, we're forced to go
As for our loss you'll never know
Slipped back when the union fell asleep
Hauled off our dead and buried them deep.

To fight against Garrad, it never will do,
Stratton and Lucas is hard to out do,
They conquered our tigers and bull pups too,
In spite of our force and all we could do."

Coffer was killed by Colonel Frye at Mill Springs. A statue is erected to Zollie Coffer at Somerset, Kentucky.

Both sides were cruel during the Civil War. Mrs. McDaniel who lives here tells a story of how her father was killed in Clay County, while eating dinner one day. Some federal soldiers drove up and asked what side he was on and upon saying the confederate side, they took him outside and shot him with a gun in his own yard.

United States. Work Projects Administration

JENNY MCKEE:

JENNY MCKEE

Mrs. Jenny McKee, of color, who lives just North of London can tell many interesting things of her life.

"Aunt Jenny" as she is called, is about eighty-five years of age, and says she thinks she is older than that as she can remember many things of the slave days. She tells of the old "masters" home and the negro shacks all in a row behind the home. She has a scar on her forehead received when she was pushed by one of the other little slaves, upon a marble mantle place and received a deep wound in her head.

The old negro lady slaves would sit in the door way of their little shacks and play with pieces of string, not knowing what else to do to pass off the time. They were never restless for they knew no other life than slavery.

Aunt Jenny McKee was born in Texas though she doesn't know what town she was born in. She remembers when her mother was sold into the hands of another slave owner, the name of the place was White Ranch Louisiana. Her mother married again, and this time she went by the name of Redman, her mother's second husband was named John Redman, and Aunt Jenny altho her real name was Jenny Garden, carried the name of Redman until she was married to McKee.

During the War her mother died with cholera, and after the war her step-father sold or gave her away to an old Negro lady by the name of Tillet, her Husband was a captain from the 116th regiment from Manchester.

They had no children and so Aunt Jenny was given or sold to Martha Tillet. Aunt Jenny still has the paper that was written with her adoption by Mrs. Martha Tillet and John Redman, the paper was exactly as written below:

White   Ranch
September 10, 1866

To Whom it may concern, I, John Redman has this day given my consent that Mrs. Martha Tillet can have my child Jenny Redman to raise and own as her child, that I shall not claim and take her away at any time in the future.

   x
John Redman
his mark

She has a picture in her possession of Captain Tillet in war costume and with his old rifle. After the war the Tillets were sent back to Manchester where he was mustered out, Aunt Jenny being with them. "I stayed with them" Aunt Jenny said, "until I was married Dec. 14, 1876, to David McKee another soldier of the 116th regiment". She draws a pension now from his services.

David McKee was a slave under John McKee, father of the late John McKee of this place. He was finally sold to a man by the name of Meriah Jackson. "David's masters were good to him" said Jenny "he learned to be a black smith under them".

Aunt Jenny has the history of the 116th regiment, U.S.C. Infantry. Tillet was captain in this regiment and David McKee a soldier then was a lot of soldiers in this regiment from here. Tom Griffin being one, a slave who died a few years ago. The history was printed in 1866 and this particular copy was presented to Captain Tillet, and bears his signature.

The first deed to be put on record in the Laurel County court was between Media Bledsoe of Garrad County of the first part and Daniel Garrard of Clay County of the second part. Being 4800 acres of land lying in Knox County on Laurel River and being that part of 16000 acres of land patented in the name of John Watts. One thousand dollars was the sum paid for this land. This is on record in Deed Book "A", page 1. Date of September 30, 1824.

United States. Work Projects Administration

JEFFERSON CO.
(BYERS YORK)

SUSAN DALE SANDERS:

SUSAN DALE SANDERS

The following is a story of Mrs. Susan Dale Sanders, #1 Dupree Alley, between Breckinridge and Lampton Sts., Louisville, an old Negro Slave mammy, and of her life, as she related it.

"I lived near Taylorsville, Kentucky, in Spencer County, nearly all my life, 'cept the last fo' or five yea's I'se been livin' here. I was bo'n there in a log cabin, it was made of logs, and it was chinked with clay and rock. My Mammy, was raised from a baby by her master, Rueben Dale. He was a good ole Master, and was alway's good to my Mammy. Master Dale owned a big farm and had big fields of co'n an' tobacco, and we raised everything we had to eat. Ole master Dale was a good ole baptist, had lots of good ole time relig'n. Ruben Dale had lots of slaves, and every family had its own cabin. As he raised my Mammy as a slave from a baby, she thought there was none livin' bett'r than her master Dale.

The next fa'm close to the Masters, was owned by a man, Colonel Jack Allen, and he had a big fa'm and owned lots of slaves. And Mammy was allowed to marry one of the Allan slaves, and my father's name was Will Allen. You see the slaves had the same name as the Master's, as he owned 'em. My Mammy had seven children and we all grow'd up on our Master Dales fa'm. My father had to stay at his master's, Col. Jack Allen's and wo'k in the fields all day, but at night he would come to my mammy's cabin and stay all night, and go back to his master's, Col. Allen's fields the next mon'in. Yes, I grow'd up in slavery times. I used to carry tubs of clothes down to the old spring house, there was plenty of water, and I'se washed all the clothes there. Me and my sisters used to wash and sing and we had a good time. I can't remember much of the ole song's its been so long ago.

I had two brothers, and they jined the war and fought in the army. One was named Harry and 'tother Peter. Mammy wo'ked hard, done all the cookin' but ole Master Dale was so good to all of us children we did't mind it. I'se was a mischevious gal when I was grow'in up. I'se would get a lickin' most every-day. I'se alway's like to fight the ot'er children, and I would say, "Mammy she hit me", but I was bad and I'se got my whipp'n. On my masters fa'm we killed a lot of hogs for our meat, had a big trough, that we cut the meat up in, and put the hams and shoulders together, and the middles together, then put 'em down in salt for about six weeks, and then hang them up in the smoke-house and smoke 'em with hickory chips. And leave them all the time till we used 'em up. We had a apple house we used to fill every fall with the best apples. The ole master sho' had a apple fa'm. Inside of the house there was a big hole in the ground, dug deep, and we use to fill it full of apples, then cover it over with a straw, and O Lawd, we would have apples all wint'r when the snow lies deep on the ground; sure I wish them old days back.

Some of the other old Masters, who had lots of slaves on fa'ms close by, was so mean to the slaves they owned. They wo'ked the women and men both in the fields and the children too, and when the ole Master thought they was'n't do'n' 'nuf wo'k, he would take his men and strip off their shirts, and lash them with cow-hide whips until you could see the blood run down them poor niggers backs.

The Nigger traders would come through and buy up a lot of men, and women slaves, and get a big drove of them and take them further south to work in the fields, leavin their babies. I'se never can forget. I know'd some mean ole masters.

Our ole master Dale that raised my Mammy and her family never was hard or mean like that. He would let us go to church, have parties and dances. One of the ole salves would come to our cabin with his fiddle and we'd dance.

After I'se grow'd up, I'se wo'ked for Mrs. Susan Lovell, that was the ole masters married daughter. She lived down the road from his fa'm. She was good to me! You see I was named after Susan Lovell. It was while I was wo'kin' fo' her when the war ended. She told me I was free after the war was over. I got happy and sung but I didn't know for a long time, what to be free was, so after the war she hired me and I stayed on doin' all the cookin' and washin' and all the work, and I was hired to her for four dollars a month. After the war was over my father died. And it wasn't long after that, I Married Wm. Sanders and we had six children. I got a Government pension, as my husband was in the army during the Civil War and he was wounded in the body, but he lived a long time after the war was ended.

In the ole days we used to sing and go to church, sing the ole time religion, and when we danced we sung: "Who's been here since I'se been gone, Ah, that gal with the blue dress on."

I'se still believes in lots of good and bad luck signs, but forget most of 'em, "But if you drap a knife, on the floor someone is sure to come to see you, and if you dream of money that is good luck." "To sneeze at the table is bad luck, to sneeze when away from the table good luck." "If you dream of the stars is bad luck."

JOHN ANDERSON:

JOHN ANDERSON

A story resulting from an interview with John Anderson, an old Negro slave:

"I was born in Pennsylvania, on Shiptown road, Clinton County, close to Mercersberg. When I was growing up my mammy always believed in making her own medicine, and doctored the whole family with the roots she dug herself. She use to bile down the roots from may-apple, snake root and blood root, and make her medicine. This was good for the blood and keep us from gettin' sick.

While the wah was goin' on, the soldiers were campin' all about us and when they heer'd the Gray's was comin' they got ready for battle, and when they did come they fit' em back, and they made their stand at Harpers Ferry, Va., and had a hard battle there. My mammy was scared of the Gray's and when she heer'd they was comin', would hide us three boys in some white folks cellar until they was gone. They would take all the young niggahs with them they could get hold of, and soon as they'd gone, we would go back home.

When the wah was over, me and some boys went over to

the battlefield and foun' a calvary gun which I had for years. We lived in a log cabin on a farm and worked for a farmer in the fields while my mammy worked in the house for the white folks. We had lots of things that is good and bad luck."

JOANA OWENS:

JOANA OWENS

The following is the life and traditions of Joana Owens, 520 E. Breckinridge St., Louisville, Kentucky, an old negro mammy who was born during slavery.

"My mother and father was slaves, and there was two children born to them, my sister and me. We used to live at Hawesville, Kentucky, on the Ohio River. My peoples name was Barr, and their masters name was Nolan Barr. You know they all had to take their masters name in slave days.

I will never forget how mean old Master Nolan Barr was to us. I was about fourteen years old and my sister was a little younger. We lived in an old log cabin. The cracks was filled with mud. My Mother done the housework for Master Barr's house. My father and sister and me had to work in the fields. He had a big farm, and owned lots of slaves, and when the old master got mad at his slaves for not working hard enough he would tie them up by their thumbs and whip the male slaves till they begged for mercy. He sure was a mean old man. I will never forget him as long as I live. I don't know exactly how old I is, but I am close to ninety now. After I growed up and married a man named Owens, we come here to Louisville to live. That was a short while after the slaves was freed. I can remember how me and my sister used to go down to the river and watch the red hospital boats come in, bringing the wounded soldiers in to be cared for, and me and sister would go long singing—Nigger—Nigger—never die, if you want a chicken pie."

[MARTHA J. JONES:]

MARTHA J. JONES

In an interview with Mrs. Martha J. Jones, she reminisced of the old Civil War days as follows:

"I was born in Buckingham County, Virginia, and later during the Civil War, I lived in Gilmer County, W. Va. My fathers name was Robert R. Turner; he was born in 1818 and my mother's name was Susan; she was born in 1821. My parents had six children and we lived on a big farm.

My father was in the legislature in W. Va. During the Civil War, I had three brother in the Southern Army. One of them died of fever, one was shot and killed in action, and the other William Wert Turner, came out of the army after the close of the war and became a lawyer. Later he went to New Castle, Kentucky, and became a prominent lawyer, where he remained until his death in 1932.

I married John R. Jones, a lieutenant in the Union Army, at Gilmer, W. Va., when I was about twenty years old, shortly after the war. We then moved to New Castle, Kentucky, Henry County. We had four children born to us, and I now have three living children; later on in years we moved to Louisville. During the days of the Civil War my father owned three slave, one was an old darkey named Alex, and the nigger mammies, were Diana and Mary Ann. My parents were always good to their slaves, and never traded or sold them. They were good workers and my father never kept many.

My Uncle, John C. Turner, had farms close to my father's in West Va., and he had fifty-two slaves when the war ended. He would buy, sell and trade them all the time. The slaves were judged by the Masters. If they were big and strong they would bring a good price, as they would be better workers for the fields, and then, I would watch my uncle swap and buy slaves, just the same as he was buying any other stock for his farm. I am getting [HW: old] now, and my memory is not so good no more, and it is hard to remember the things of so long ago. You see, I will be ninety years old, next Feb. 23rd. I was born in 1847."

FLOYD CO.
(JOHN I. STURGILL)

CHARLIE RICHMOND:

CHARLIE RICHMOND

We are unable to interview ex-slaves in Floyd County, so far as anyone we are able to contact knows, there are no living ex-slaves in the County. There are several colored people. The majority of them reside at Tram, Kentucky, Floyd County, in a kind of colored colony, having been placed there just after the Civil War. A small number of colored people live in the vicinity of Wayland, Kentucky, the original being the remains of a wealthy farmer of Civil War day, by name of Martin. The colored people were identified as "Martin's Niggers."

The last ex-slave of Floyd County, says Mr. W.S. Wallen of Prestonsburg, Kentucky, was "Uncle" Charlie Richmond, of Prestonsburg. Uncle Charlie was brought to the county by old Judge Richmond, father of I. Richmond of the Richmond Dept. Stores of Prestonsburg, about the time of the Civil War. When the war was over "Uncle" Charlie worked at Richmond's for hire and lived as a member of the family. While working on a Prestonsburg newspaper,

Mr. Wallen interviewed this old ex-slave and worked him into a feature story for his paper. These old paper files were destroyed by fire about 1928.

Mr. Wallen remembers that "Uncle" Charlie Richmond, as the old ex-slave was called, died in 1910, was buried in Prestonsburg, and that he, W.S. Wallen, wrote up the old Darkey's death and funeral for his newspaper. This is the same paper who's files were destroyed by fire and which papers does not now exist.

Old Judge Richmond brought this old slave, from Virginia about 1862, along with a number of other slaves. "Uncle" Charlies was the only slave that remained in the family as a servant after the Emancipation Proclamation.

Mr. Wallen is a lawyer in Prestonsburg, Kentucky, a member of the James and Wallen Law Firm, located in the Lane Bldg., on Court St. He was born at Goodlow, Kentucky in Floyd County, March 15, 1866. He taught school in Floyd County thirteen years, took his L.L.B. at Law School in Valpariso, Ind., in 1910, and later served as representative to the Kentucky General Assembly from the 93rd District, the 1922-24 and 26 Sessions.

The List of People who owned Slaves in Floyd County include:

Sophia Lane, Lanesville.

Jim Lane, Lanesville

Gilbert Higgins, Wilson's Creek

George May, Maytown

Hi Morgan, Prestonsburg

Penny J. Sizemore, Prestonsburg

Samuel P. Davidson, Prestonsburg

I. Richmond, Prestonsburg

Valentine Mayo, Prestonsburg

---- Lanes, Prestonsburg

Kennie Hatcher, Lanesville

Morgan Clark, John's Creek

Daniel Hager, Hager Shoals near what is Auxier, Ky.

Adam Gayheart, Prestonsburg

John P. Martin, Prestonsburg

Jacob Mayo, Sr., Prestonsburg

Wm. Mayo, Jr., Prestonsburg

Johnny Martin, Wayland, Kentucky

Thomas Johns, Dwale, Ky.

Isom Slone, Beaver Creek

John Bud Harris, Emma, Kentucky

Billy Slone, Caney Fork, Right Beaver, Kentucky.

This list is as remembered by the oldest citizens, and one T.J. "Uncle" Jeff Sizemore, 94 years old Civil War Veteran and citizen of Prestonsburg, Kentucky, dictated then to the writer in just this order.

The nearest auction blocks were Mt. Sterling, Kentucky and Gladdville, Virginia. Most slaves from the present Floyd County Territory were bought and sold through auction in southwest Virginia. Other auction blocks were at Abington and Bristol, Virginia.

The negro dialect of this county is a combination of the dialect white folk use plus that of the negro of the South. The colored population is continually moving back and forth from Alabama, Georgia and North and South Carolinas. They visit a lot. Colored teachers so far have all been from Ohio. Most visiting colored preachers come from Alabama and the Carolinas. The negroes leave out their R's use an't han't gwin, su' for sir, yea for yes, dah for there and such expressions as, "I's Ye?"

The wealthiest families o' white folk still retain colored servants. In Prestonsburg, Kentucky one may see on the streets neat looking colored gals leading or wheeling young white children along. Folk say this is why so many southerners leave out their R's and hold on to the old superstitions, they've had a colored mama for a nursemaid.

Adam Gearheart was a sportsman and used negro Jockeys. His best jockey, Dennis, was sold to Morg. Clark, John's

Creek. The old race track took in part of the east end of the present Prestonsburg—from Gearheart's home East in Mayo's bottom one mile to Kelse Hollow—Jimmie Davidson now lives at the beginning of the old track, near Maple Street. Mike Tarter of Tennessee, Gearheart's son-in-law brought horses from Tennessee and ran them here. Tarter was a promoter and book-maker also. Penny J. Sizemore and Morg. Clark were other sportsmen. This was as early as 1840 up to the Civil War.

Slaves ware traded, bought and sold between owners just as domestic animals are today. Where one owned only a few servants with no families they lived in the big house—otherwise in Slave quarters, little cabins nearby.

Billy Slone just had two female servants, he bought them in Virginia 15 years old, for $1,000.00 sound.

Many folk went over to Mt. Sterling or Lexington to auctions for trading servants. (The same manner is used trading stock today).

Slave traders came into the county to buy up slaves for the Southern plantations, and cotton or sugar fields—Slave families were very frequently separated, some members mean, theiving, or running away niggers were sold (first) down the river. Sometimes good servants were sold for the price, the master being in a financial strait or dire need of money. Traders handcuffed their servants purchased, and took them by boat or horse-back down the river or over in Virginia and Carolina tobacco fields.

Good servants were usually well treated and not overworked. Mean or contrary servants were whipped, or punished in other ways. Run-aways were hunted—dogs being used to track them at times.

OWENS CO.
(JOHN FORSEE)

GEORGE DORSEY:

GEORGE DORSEY

Although this article is presented in narrative form and has but few characters, the writer believes it to be an excellent example of life in Owen County sixty or more years ago. With the exception of the grey eagle episode, similar events to these described were happening all over the county. There is no reason to doubt the authenticity of any part of the article. The narrator (George Dorsey, age 76 (negro) Owentown, Kentucky, born in slavery and raised by a white family) bears a good reputation and is intelligent enough to react favorably and intelligently to questions concerning the past. Further interviews concerning more general subjects are planned.

"I was born on the 16th day of June, 1860 on the ole poor house farm 'bout two miles from Owentown. My mother yousta tell me I'd be a sleepy head. I didn't know what she meant by that so finally one day, after I got to be a great big boy, I asked her what she meant.

"Well, she says, Chickens that is hatched in June jess

stand 'round in the hot sun an' sleep themselves to death. So, as you was born in June, you'll jess be a sleepy head."

"My mother belonged to Sammy Duvall, the father o' little Sam Duvall who died not long ago. Little Sam usta be town marshall here and a guard at the pen over at Frankfort. I was born a slave an' stayed one till the niggers was freed.

"Bout the time the war was over I seen my first soldier. The road that passed along in front of our house was a dirt road. I'd gone with mother to watch her milk a young cow late one night, 'bout dark I guess, when I heard somebody hollerin' and yellin' an' I looked down the road an' seen 'em comin'. I was 'bout five years old then an' it looked to me like all the army was comin' up the road. The captain was on a hawse an' the men afoot an' the dust from the dirt road a flyin'. There was a moon shinin' an' you could see the muskets shinin' in the moonlight. I was settin' on a fence an' when I seen 'em it scared me so I started to run. When I jumped off I fell an' cut a hole in my for'head right over this left eye. The scar's there yet. I run in the house and hid. Mr. Sammy Duvall had to get on a hawse an' go to New Liberty an' fetch a doctor to plug up the hole in my head. I seen lots of soldiers after that an' I always run under the bed or hid in a closet or somewheres. They stayed 'round here for a long time. Finally provender got low and the soldiers took to stealing. We called it stealin', but I reckon it warn't for they come and got the stuff like meat out o' the smoke house in broad open daylight. Mr. Duvall had a chestnut earl stallion he called Drennon an' they come, or somebody did, an' got him one night. One day, 'bout two or three weeks later, Will Duvall, a son o' Mr. Sammy Duvall, heard that the hawse was over in Henry County where the soldiers had a camp. So he went over there and found the Captain an' told him he'd come after old Drennon. The Captain said to describe him an' Will said, "Captain, he's a chestnut earl named Drennon. If'n I whistl' a certain way he' nicker an' answer me."

"Well, they went down to the stable where they had a lot of stalls like, under tents. An' when they got there, Will, he whistled, an' sure 'nough, old Drennon nickered. So the Captain, he said, That's your hawse all right. Go in an' get him an' take him on home.

Will brought the hawse home an' took him down in the woods on the creek where the water'd washed all the dirt offen a big, flat rock and we kep him hid for three or four weeks. We didn't want to loose him again.

When I was 'bout six years old we moved offen the creek to a new road up on the ridge. It was on the same farm but to another house. I had a great big, ole grey cat I called "Tom." I wanted to move him so I put him in a pillow slip so's he couldn't see where we wus takin' him so he couldn't fin' the way back. He stayed 'round his new home for a few days an' then he went back to his ole home. Mr. Duvall went and got him again for me. Not many white men would do that for a little nigger boy. He musta told Tom somethin' for he never run off no more.

Mr. Duvall usta ride a blazed-face, sarl [HW: sorrel] mare named Kit. He most al'ays taken me up behind him, 'specially if he was goin' to town. Kit was trained to hunt deer. I can't remember any deer in the country but Mr. Duvall yousta tell me 'bout 'em an 'bout the way they had their hawses trained. He said there wus a place down on

Panther Lick Creek, below where we lived, that was a deer lick. The deer would come there and lick the ground close to the creek because there was salt left there by the high waters. He'd put a strap with a littel bell on 'round ole Kit's neck; an' tie her to a tree not far from this lick. Then he'd hide behin' 'nother tree close to Kit. When the deer come ole Kit'd shake her head an' the deer would raise their heads to see what the noise made by the bell was an' where it was comin' from. Then he'd shoot the deer in the head. He showed me the place where he killed the biggest buck he ever seen right here jess out o' town a little ways. He kept the horns. An' I remember seein' 'em in the attic at his house. He had an ole riffle he called "Ole Betsy" that'd been his deer rifle.

After I got to be a big boy, huntin' and fishin' was good. I never got to do any uv it except on Saturdays and Sundays. Everbody had a brush fence 'round the house to keep the stock in out o' the yard and one day I seen a big bird sail down on the fence and run under it. Mother was out in the back yard so I said to myself, I'll get the gun and kill that hawk. I taken good aim at its head and banged away. At the crack o' the gun I never heard such a flutterin' in my life. Mother come runnin' to see what was the matter and when she seen it, she said, Son, that's a pheasant. Some day you'll be a good hunter. An' guess I was for I killed lots o' pheasants, quail, squir'ls and rabbits.

Little Sammy Duvall had a pointer he called "Quail". She was the smartest dog I ever seen, but everybody had smart dogs them days. Quail'd trail birds when they was runnin' till she got clost and then circle 'round 'em an' make her stand.

Be careful there, Quail, Mr. Sammy would say. He'd

nearly always get eight or ten out uv a covey an' sometimes the whole covey. I yousta go along jess to see him shoot. He hardly ever missed. There was so many quail that nobody ever thought to leave any uv a covey if he wanted that many an' they didn't get so scattered that he couldn't fin' em.

After the deer was all killed out, people trained their deer hounds to chase foxes, coons and such like. The white boys from town yousta come and get Will and young Sammy to go coon huntin'. They al'ays had ten or twelve dogs. They al'ays taken me along an' treated me jest the same as if I was as white as they was. If I got behind or out o' sight somebody was sure to say, 'Where's George'?

One night we treed three coons in a big hollow oak. They started to cut down the trees an' put me at the butt with a fire bran'. When the tree fell the coons'd come out an' I was supposed to drive 'em back with the fire, jest lettin' out one at a time so's the dogs could kill 'em. I was about half scared uv 'em and when one big feller come out I backed up an' he got by me. I throwed the fire at him an' it lit on his back an' burnt' him. I never seen a coon run so fast. But the dogs soon treed him again an' we got him. Then we come back an' the dogs picked up the trail uv another one an' we catched him. I never seed a bigger one. He was as long as this umbrella (3-1/2 ft.) The other one got away. Coon huntin' was a great sport with the boys an' men in those days.

I catched the only grey eagle that was ever seen 'round here. They was a bunch of us boys out rabbit huntin' one day one fall. The dogs got after a rabbit an' chased it across a holler out o' range. I had the only gun in the crowd an' was right after that rabbit. The dogs run over the track an' could see 'em over on the hillside jess settin' still. All at once I seen a big bird—I taken it to be a hawk, fold its wings like a man'd fold his arms 'round his body, and drop straight down on the rabbit. But the rabbit saw it too for when the eagle got there he was ten feet up the hillside. The bird hit, "boom", jest like that. But the rabbit was goin' over the hill an' the eagle musta saw him for he riz an' flew in that direction.

'You boys stay back, I'll kill that hawk. That's the biggest hawk I ever seen,' I told them. When I got to the top of the ridge I seen him settin' in the top uv a big tree. The boys stayed where I told them and I slipped along till I got pritty close enough to shoot him. He was either watchin' the rabbit or didn't think I was watchin' him for I got pritty close before he started to fly. Jess as he opened his wings I let him have it with my old muzzle loader shotgun. Down he come makin' as much noise as a whole flock o' hawks oughta made. He was alive when I got to him an' made right at me, strikin' with his claws an' bill. The dogs come when they heard the shot an' he whipped 'em off. Every time he struck one of 'em he (the dog) would holler like he'd been speared. The other boys wanted to kill it but I gotta a long pole an' got it on him so's it held him down. We'd found out by this time that one wing was broke by my shot. So we jess hold of the tips of his wings an' led him to the house. His wing spread was 'bout six or eight feet. When I got him to the house I told 'em I had the biggest hawk they ever seen. A ole man by the same of William said, "Hell that ain't no hawk, that's a grey eagle." A ole colored fiddler, named Fred Roberts, sent word he'd buy it from me. He even got so fraid he wouldn't get it that he come for it.

'What'll you take for him', he asked me, and before I could say anything he says, 'I'll give a dollar for him'.

That was a lot of money for me an' boy like I sold him then and there. I coulda got two or maybe three dollars for him. Fred taken him to town an' fed him live hens and raw meat. On court days or when there was a crowd in town he showed him for ten cents a look. I bet he made $50.00 on him. People yousta to come for miles to see that eagle. He finally died.

Fishin' was good too. We cut our poles in the woods an' used to flax thread for lines. Where people built water-gaps in fences that crossed the creeks the water'd fill in till it made a dam. Then the creek spread behind it. Them water holes was full o1 perch an' cat fish. They didn't get much bigger them your hand but they bit fast and we had lots o' fun catchin' 'em.

United States. Work Projects Administration

CHRISTIAN CO.
(MAMIE HANBERRY)

ANNIE B. BOYD:

ANNIE B. BOYD

[TR: Interviewer's name also spelled also spelled Hanbery.]

Annie B. Boyd, born August 22nd 1851, resides at corner of Liberty and First Street, Hopkinsville, Kentucky. Born a slave belonging to Charles Cammack near Gordonsville, Kentucky in Christian County. "My mother and me war put on de block in front of de Courthouse in Hopkinsville and sold to Mr. Newt. Catlett and we brung $500.00. Marse Catlett lived on the corner of Seventh and Clay Streets, Hopkinsville, Kentucky. Wen I was older the white folks had me foh to nurse dar chilluns. I noes wen de war broke out marse had a store and den marsa took me to his wife's kinfolks down in de country till freedom war declared den my stepfather come an' got me. Of course I hed ter work and den I went ter nurse foh Dr. Fairleigh and nussed his daughter Madge. De white folks wont good to me. My marster was a good man but my missus wont no good woman. She uster box my ears, stick pins in me and tie me ter de cedar chest and whoop me as long as she wanter. Oh, how I did hate dat woman.

"Yes, once in my life I seed a ghost. We was goin' thru de woods to a neighbors ter a prayer meeting en a man stepped out in de woad without no head wid all his clothes on en I had jes wropped my head dat day and wen I seed him all my hair strings en all jes stood straight up. I got hot den I'se got cold and he jest stepped ter de side of de road en I went by running. Yes, we got ter de prayer meeting en den we went back home de same way en did us niggers run?

"I was nurse in slave time en I carried de chilluns all ober de house en one day I had de chilluns upstars en my missus called me en I went ter see whar she wont and while I'se war gone de baby got hodter Indian Turnip an hed bit it by de time I git back dar en I called my missus en she come en made me eat de rest of de turnip en my face enall swelled up en my eyes war closed foh days. After missing de baby en tending ter de uther chilluns all de day an night wen I put de baby ter bed I bed ter knit two round ebery night en would be sleepy en my missus would reach ober en jab a pin in me to keep me awake. Now dat is what I calls a mean woman.

"I kin read en write at first of freedom I sent ter school some en learned ter read and write.

"I sho do believe in dreams. I had one once I laid down on de bed ter take er nap en den I dreamed dat somethin was a chokin me en I pulled at my dress en a big snake dropped out of my bosom rolled down on de bed. Den on de floor en when I woke up sho nuff dar war a snake on de floor by de bed en I killed it en den I knowed dat I had an enemy sho nuff in a few days a woman I thot was my friend turned gain me. By killing de snake I knowed dat I would conquer dat enemy.

"I noes wishes cen come tru seems ter me I hev but my memory aint so good but still I believes hit.

"Wen de smoke flies low hit sho is goin ter snow."

"Spilling salt or ter waste salt is bad luck. I always wen I makes my bread put de salt in de bread den I puts some of de salt in de fire ter bring me good luck.

"Sometime de moon affects people wen it changes hit makes some folks crazy en dey is hard to git alon wid."

"If you plant Irish pertatoes on de light of de moon you hev nuthin but top. Whatever ter be made underneath de ground like turnips, potatoes, onions is ter be planted by de dark of de moon. Beans, peas, corn in de light of de moon.

"Yes, spit will cure, cause I had ringworms once en in de morning wen I woke up afore I spoke ter anyone I'd take spit en put on my face en hit sho cured de ringworms."

(Signs)

"If you nail a horse shoe ober de door hits a good luck ter you.

"I thin "13" is an unlucky number I'se heard so much talk of hit till I believes hit. Breaking a mirror is sho bad luck if you break one you will hev seben years bad luck."

"Blue gummed niggers is shon bad luck wen I sees one

gits as far away as I kin foh if one bites you you is a ded nigger foh dey is pizen as er diamond back."

"De white folks jes made niggers carry on like brutes. One white man uster say ter nuther white man, "My nigger man Sam wanter marry yer nigger gal Lucy what does yer say en if he said hit war all right why dat couple war supposed to be married. Den Sam would work foh his marster in de daytime en den would spend de night at Lucy's house on de next plantation."

KATE BILLINGSBY:

KATE BILLINGSBY

Kate Billingsby, Ex-slave, according to a record in a Bible the Buckners gave her when she married was born in 1828. She was owned by Frank and Sarah Buckner. Born in this County and has spent her life in and around Hopkinsville. She lives on what is known as the Gates Mill Road about one half mile east of US 41E and owns her own home.

Aunt Kate as she is generally called is a small black negro and in going into her home you will find it furnished in lovely antique furniture in a disreputable state of repair. She met me with a dignity and grace that would be a credit to any one of the white race to copy, illiterate though she may be. Her culture and training goes back to the old Buckner family, at one time one of the most cultured families in Christian County. She is not a superstitious negro. Being born a Buckner slave, she was never sold and her manners and ways proclaim that she surely must have been raised in "De white folks house" as she claims, being a maid when old enough, to one of Frank Buckner's daughters. She stated, "Dese Buckners war sho good to me, eben now dey chilluns comes to see me and always bring me something. Dey don let my taxes lapse am I'se neber widout somting to eat." My man and I was married by Mr. Alexander at McClain College. I was de cook an he was the janitor. My man followed his Massa in de Secess War. If he was a livin' now he would be 110 years old, he bin ded 'round fifteen year."

No I'se done believe in no ghosts hants or anything of that kind my white folks being "quality". I'se been raised by "quality"! Why I'se "quality nigger". "Wen any of my folks git sick or eny of my white folks de doctor would always bee sent foh." (Her address is: R.R. #2, Hopkinsville, Ky.)

NANNIE EAVES:

NANNIE EAVES

Nannie Eaves, age 91, born in McLain County, Ky. being a slave of William Eaves, never sold, address now R.R. #2, Hopkinsville, Kentucky.

"I guess I was about twenty one years old wen I was freed." I'se was neber once treated as a slave cause my Massa was my very own Daddy. Ben Eaves my husband was a slave en chile of George Eaves my Massa's brother. He ran away from his Massa en his Daddy en jins the U.S. Army during the Secess War en I'se now drawing a pension from Uncle Sam. I'se sho glad dat he had sense nuff ter go dis way or I'd be jes like dese old niggers dat is now on de Government.

"Course I never sweep de trash out de house after sun down jest sweep hit in de corner of de room cause hit is bad luck ter sweep out de door after dark. Lawd yes squeech owls en dogs howling under de house shi God means dar is going ter be a death in de family. Wen I hears one I'se git trembly all ober, hit makes me hot en den cold both de same time."

"Ho I haint neber seed a ghost or hant but I sho don wanter see one neither. I'se always fraid I will seed one.

Sho de dead can hant you if war not good to dem wen dey is livin'. Signs en sech things is going out of style now but Lor wen I was a chile why seems like things war better cause of dem."

Nannie is a tall bright negro holding herself very straight, with real white long hair. Her hair is very fine and wavy. Her cabin home was immaculate, furnished very neatly in the now prevailing style.

Slave Trades: "We had two slave traders in this town. They were Judge Houston and his son-in-law, Dr. Brady. They gathered up all the slaves that were unrully or that people wanted to trade and housed them in an old barn until they had enough to take to New Orleans on a boat. They traded them down there for work in the cotton fields.

MARY WRIGHT:

MARY WRIGHT

Mary Wright, 204 W. Fourth St., Born August 1, 1865.

"I was born at Gracey, Kentucky on Mr. James Colemans far, in a log cabin wid a dirt floor en a stick chimney.

"Folks uster weat wat dey calls a "Polanaise". Hid wat kinder like a wrapper made of calico made wid tight in de waist en wide in de bottom. Den I've remembers de basque waist on de over skirts dese war made real tight waists wid a point in de back en ober de stomach. De skirt wer real full dem a skirt ober dis ter de knees wid a big pucker on de hips."

"My Mammy bound me out to Miss Puss Graham ter learn ter work, foh my vittals en cloes. Miss Puss gave me a pair of red morocco shoes en I was made so happy, I'se neber fohgot dese shoes.

"I heard my Mammy talk of "De Nigger Risin". De Klu Klux uster stick de niggers head on er stake alongside de Cadiz road en dar de buzzards would eat them till nuthin' was left but de bones. Dar war a sign on dis stake dat said "Look out Nigger You are next". Us chilluns would not go far way from dat cabin. I'se tells you dat is so. I jes knowed dat dis Ku Klux would do dat to us sho if weuns had been catched.

"I remember wen Hopkinsville had jest a few stores en ole jew by name of Shyer bought bones an iron en rags. Once us chilluns found some bones on de creek bank en took dem things and wanted ter sell dem to Mr. Shyer en he said 'take dem things way dey stink, dey aint cured up yet. Bury dem things den bring dem back to me. Us Chilluns bed a hard time gittin home cause we stunk so bad.'

"I remember wen we uster hev big time quilting on dem days we sho had a big time fore we start in de morning wid a water melon feast, den weuns quilt erwhile den a big dinner war spread out den after dinner we'd quilt in the evening den supper and a big dance dat night, wid de banjo a humming en us niggers a dancing, "Oh, Lawdy wat good days dem war."

"Wen we were young we uster hev parties called "Dideoos", de banjo would play en den de girls would line up on one side of de cabin en de boys on de tother side while the folks war a clappin en er playing why de boys en girls wuld choose dar parrners den weuns sing:

> "Ole Brer Rabbit,
> Shake it, shake it,
> How I love you,
> Shake it, shake it.

I'd ruther play dat game dan to eat."

"We uster tap maple trees en hev big gathering foh ter make maple sugar dat war while I lived at Gracey.

"De stage coach day war big days, wen de stage coach war a comin thru why us little niggers would try ter keep up wid de horses en run erlong side de coach en sometimes a man or woman would drop us a penny den dar was sho a scramble."

"I remember wen we uster wash cloes wid a paddle. You wet dese cloes en put soft soap in dem, the soap war made outer ash lye en grease den dese cloes war spread on a smooth stump an beat wid paddles till dey war clean. Den come de wooden wash board, hit war jes a piece of wood wid rough places or ridges chiseled in hit. Wen we uster wash quilts we uster cyt a nikasses varrek ubter eb dat made de tub deb my Mammy would put water in dese tubs den soft soap de quilts den us chilluns would git in de tubs in our Bare foots en tromp de dirt out."

"We uster use grease lamps, dese war made outer iron, wid a piece of cotton rope down in de grease on dis jes send out a puny smelly light. Dem de brass lamp came erlong hit war a little lamp wid a wich wid a handle in er stem, no burner or nuthin hit burned coaloil but had no chimney."

"Hee, Hee, Hee, I remember arbout a story Mary Beard told ter me erbout a slave woman dat war foolish. Her Massa couldn't git no body ter buy her, hee, hee, hee, so he dresses her up nice en buys her a thimble en gives her a piece of cloth ter sew on. It war right here in Hopkinsville in front of de court house dat de block war en he sold dis woman as a "sewing slave", en her war foolish en couldn't take er right stitch en she sho brought a good price en wen her new Massa found out she war foolish he sho war mad. He tried ter sell her but pshaw he bought something he couldn't git rid of, Hee, Hee."

"Dese ole nigger slave traders uster so my Mammy said, steal de niggers from one Massa and dey would leave at night en stay in "Campbells Cave" den dey would take dese niggers wid a promise of freedom to Clarksville, Tenn., sell dem again on "Mr. Dunk Morr's" slave market. Sometimes dese niggers if dey got a new Massa dat war mean would run erway en come back tar dar ole Massas."

"Yes I believe you can be hauted, I aint neber seed one tho but I'se heard dem en I jest git creepy en I no's dey is around."

"Cos dreams come tru, I dont remember one now but if I'se had one ergin I will try ter remember en tells you."

"No I aint neber seed a ghost. I feels dem sometimes en I jis shot my eyes en pray de "Good Lawd" ter send dat ghost away."

"If youse find a horse shoe er put eber de door you will sho has good luck."

"Thirteen has always been my lucky number. Dats follish ter thing 'Thirteen is unlucky'. Seben is lucky ter me ter. I always win when I think of a seben."

"Of cos now if youse breakes a mirror you cant keep from having bad luck. Nuthin you do will keep you from hit."

"Sho is bad luck ter meet a cross-eyed pusson er blue gummed niggers is pizen cause if one bites you youse will sho ter die."

"My Mammy sho did hev a big wedding my Pappys Massa ask my Mammy Massa foh her en den my Mammy Massa give her a big infair dat cost him $200.00 wid de bridal supper en all."

"Dey uster do niggers pretty bad erbout dat funerals. Wen a nigger did die why de rest of de niggers hed ter work en one nigger made de box whiler ernother nigger dug de grave en the nigger war jes civered up en den on de Fourth Sunday in August ebery year all de colored folks would take a basket dinner ter de church en each family dat had buried a nigger would pay de preacher ter preach the sermon foh dat darkie dat died. We ate dinner en supper at de church en sometimes the funeral foh some fo de darkies wouldn't git preached till next August. We went to dis funeral why we had big time talking wid our neighbors en of de dead."

"Dogs howling meand bad luck if he howls under de house why someone is goin ter die."

"If er owl come around de house on holler a death will happen in de family fore de next day."

"I remembers I wat a sitting in de house en er peckerwood war a pecking on de house 'Pure bad luck.'"

"I was working once foh Mrs. Shelton wen a little wren kept trying ter git in de house an I kep a shosin hit arway wen he got in somehow jes as soon as hit did Mrs. Shelton called me en I had a telegram from Chicago my neice war dead. She by dat I nos dat am bad luck. I dont like wrens any how."

"Wenn a cow loses hits cud, jes giv hit an old dirty dish rag en den de cow will ding her cud again."

"Sometimes a cow gits sich en lay down en if you will fell her tail on de end it is all soft, 'Dat cow hot holler tail, en less you split dat tail en fill de holler wid salt den bind hit up dat cow will sholy die.'"

"I asked Mary if she was superstitious and she said 'no, cos niggers are edicatted dese days en dey don believe in all dat tom-foolery. Dey neber would benn so foolish if de white folks did not tell us all dat rot.'" Mary neither reads or writes and is not superstitious according to her admission. What do you think of it. I am afraid that I do not agree with. M.D.H.)

CLAY CO.
(PEARL HOUSE)

SOPHIA WORD:

SOPHIA WORD

The following story of slave days is the exact words of one who had the bitter experience of slavery. Sophia Word, who is now ninety-nine years of age, born February 2, 1837. She tells me she was in bondage for nineteen years and nine months. I shall repeat just as she told the story:

"I wuz here in time of Mexican War and seed 'em get up volunteers to go. They wuz dressed in brown and band played 'Our Hunting Shirts are Fringed with Doe and away We march to Mexico'.

"My grandmother came straight from Africa and wuz auctioned off and bought by William Reide Father. When he died William Reides inherited my mother. Mother married a Bates and had ten of us children.

"Our Master didn't auction off his slaves as the other masters would for he was a better master than most of them. When he started to sale one of us he would go out and talk to the old slave trader like he wuz g'wine to sale a cow or sometin and then he would come back to git the slave he wanted. This wuz the way my mothers' brother and sister wuz sold. When the other masters at other places sold a slave they put the slave on the auction block and the slave trader had a long whop that he hit them with to see if they could jump around and wuz strong. The largest and brought the money.

"I wuz a slave nineteen yeahs and nine months but somehow or nuther I didn't belong to a real mean pet of people. The white folks said I was the meanest nigger that ever wuz. One day my Mistress Lyndia called fer me to come in the house, but no, I wouldn't go. She walks out and says she is Gwine make me go. So she takes and drags me in the house. Then I grabs that white woman, when she turned her back, and shook her until she begged for mercy. When the master comes in, I wuz given a terrible beating with a whip but I did'nt care fer I give the mistress a good'un too.

"We lived off to the back of the masters house in a little log cabin, that had one winder in the side. We lived tobly well and didn't starve fer we had enough to eat but we didn't have as good as the master and mistress had. We would slip in the house after the master and mistress wuz sleeping and cook to suit ourselves and cook what we wanted.

"The Mistress had an old parrot and one day I wuz in the kitchen making cookies, and I decided I wanted some of them so I tooks me out some and put them on a chair and when I did this the mistress entered the door, I picks up a cushion and throws over the pile of cookies on the chair and mistress cane near the chair and the old parrot cries out, Mistress burn, Mistress burn, then the mistress looks under the cushion and she had me whupped but the next day I killed the parrot, and she often wondered who or what killed the bird.

"I've seen whole pigs roasted before open fire place and when it wuz done we would put a nice red apple in its mouth and the big white folks company that come would eat of this delicious dish. Sometimes we had to bake pies for a week to supply the company that wuz invited to our masters and mistresses house. They served elaborate dinners and hundreds of guest were invited.

"My master wuzn't as mean as most masters. Hugh White was so mean to his slaves that I know of two gals that killt themselfs. One nigger gal sudie wuz found across the bed with a pen knife in her hand. He whipped another nigger gal most to death fer fergiting to put onions in the stew. The next day she went down to the river and fer nine days they searched fer her and her body finally washed upon the shore. The master could never live in that house again as when he would go to sleep he would see the nigger standing over his bed. Then he moved to Richmond and there he stayed until a little later when he hung himself.

"Our clothes wuz made from cotton and linsey. Cotton wuz used in the summer and linsey fer the winter. Sometimes our clothes wuz yeller checked and most time red. Our stockings wuz made of coarse yarn fer winter to wear with coarse shoes. We had high topped shoes fer Sunday.

"I've seed ten thousand of the Union Soldiers and a great many of the rebel soldiers. The Rebel soldiers would take everything they could get their hands on but I never did know of the Union Soldier taking anything. The rebels have stole my masters cows and horses and we would have to hide the meat in a box and bury it in the ground."

BOYD CO.
(CARL F. HALL)

CARL F. HALL

The Commonwealth of Kentucky, having for a northern boundary the Ohio River—the dividing line between the northern free states and the southern slave states has always been regarded as a southern state. As in the other states of the old south, slavery was an institution until the Thirteenth Ammendment to the Constitution of the United States gave the negro freedom in 1865.

Kentucky did not, as other southern states, secede from the Union, but attempted to be neutral during the Civil War. The people, however, were divided in their allegience, furnishing recruits for both the Federal and Confederate armies. The president of the Union, Abraham Lincoln, and the president of the Confederacy, Jefferson Davis, both were born in this state.

Boyd County was formed in 1860 from parts of Lawrence, Greenup and Carter Counties, and we are unable to find any records, in Boyd County, as to slave holders and their slaves, though it is known that many well to do families the Catletts, Davis, Poages, Williams and others were slave holders.

Slaves were not regarded as persons, had no civil rights and were owned just as any other chattel property, were bought and sold like horses and cattle, and knew no law but the will of their white masters and like other domestic animals could be, and were, acquired and disposed of without regard to family ties or other consideration.

Usually, as each slave represented a large investment of money, they were well cared for, being adequately fed, clothed and sheltered, having medical attention when sick.

As, along the border in Kentucky, there were no large plantations where field workers could be used, most of the slaves in this region were house servants, who were housed in wings of the master's house, where the plantations were large enough to need many slaves, they were furnished one, or two, rooms cabins close by the mansion on the master's estate.

As educated people are apt to be able to figure out ways to improve their lot, learning among the negroes was not encouraged, in fact it was illegal to teach them. In some instances an enlighted and humane master would teach a servant, and often they could find some one who would teach them secretly. As a race, however, they were, at the time they were set free, without any education at all.

Tales are told of cruel masters who overworked, flogged and otherwise mistreated their helpers and slaves; these masters, however, seem to have been an exception to the rule and considering that they were generally well provided for, many slaves were better off economically than the laborer of today who is a victim of misfortunes such as sickness, disability and old age.

One reason why slaves were better treated here than further south, was that Kentucky was a border state, and throughout Ohio and other northern states, was an organization known as the "Underground Railroad." This was a sort of secret society whose members were sworn to assist escaped slaves to run away to Canada where they would be free. When a run-away slave crossed the Ohio River he would be met by some one of this organization and taken where he could remain in hiding by day, then by traveling by night, could reach another place of concealment by morning, where he would be fed and hidden until darkness permitted him to reach the next haven. By this means many were successful in reaching freedom, though they were hunted by officers, armed with guns, and assisted by fierce dogs especially trained for this work.

Negroes who were unruly, or were caught attempting to escape, were usually sold to planters in the far south where they could not hope to escape, and were forced to end their days in unremitting toil in the cotton and cane fields, forever separated from relatives and friends.

It was the barbarism practiced by cruel masters, so vividly portrayed in such books as "Uncle Tom's Cabin" and songs like "Nellie Gray," that awakened the nation's conscience and brought about the bloody "Civil War" which resulted in the race being set free.

Just before the war, George Davis, a mulatto, son of his master and a black servant girl, was in Cincinnati and was accosted by two white men who offered to use the good offices of the "Underground Railroad" to help him to get away to Canada. Being well treated, as a trusted servant of his white father and master, he did not avail himself of this opportunity to escape and stayed on as a slave until Freed by the war, after which he went to Ohio and settled and prospered until his death.

Another slave, Asberry Parker, did escape, and traveling by night hiding by day, reached safety in Canada where he worked and saved until he became wealthy. After the war, when he could safely return to the United States, he moved to Ironton, Ohio, where he made his home for the rest of his life. He belonged in his days of slavery, to a Williams family, in Carter County, Kentucky.

Another slave, George McVodie, belonging to the Poage family, of Boyd Co., escaped and went to Canada, no [TR: missing word?] as to whether he ever came back later.

A sister of George Davis was sold to a planter in Louisiana where she lived until 1877, when she returned to Boyd County as a free woman.

As negroes, in slavery days, were regarded as beasts of burden not much interest was taken in the welfare of their souls. Some kind hearted masters would allow them the privilege of meeting in religious service, where some one of their race in spite of the conditions of the times, could read and explain the Bible, would preach. Other masters would not allow this to be done. A negro would become, in character much like the family who owned him, i.e., an honest, moral and kindly master would have slaves of like qualities, while a cruel, dishonest master would usually affect his slaves so that they would be tricky and unreliable.

Where the master did not personally supervise his slaves and left them to the mercies of a hired "over-seer," their lot was usually much worse, as these task-masters were almost always tyranical and were not restrained by a sense of ownership from abusing the helpless creatures under their authority as were the master's, whose money was invested in them.

On one occasion, a young negro saw his own sister stripped naked and unmercifully whipped by one of these over-seers. He gathered up all of his small belongings and tied them in a bundle and securing a club of wood, laid in wait for the cruel 'boss' until dark, when he killed him with the club. He then escaped, via the "Underground Railroad."

One thing he was careful to do, was to avoid all telegraph poles, as that he thought the wires could detect and betray him, the telegraph was a mystery to his ignorant mind. He succeeded in making his way to Canada and freedom where he stayed until after the war, when it was safe to return.

The slave trade of importing slaves into the United States, being forbidden after about 1820, cut off the supply to such an extent that strong, healthy negroes became very high in price. Many Kentucky slave owners raised slaves for this market just as we today raise live stock on our farms.

Only the strong healthy slave women were allowed to have children, and often were not allowed to mate with their own husbands, but were bred like live stock to some male negro who was kept for that purpose because of his strong phisique, which the master wished to reproduce, in order to get a good price for his progeny, just like horses, cattle, dogs and other animals are managed today in order to improve the stock. Often the father of a comely black woman's child, would be the master himself, who would heartlessly sell his own offspring to some other master, without regard for his welfare.

Many of the aristocratic women of the master class, to keep from the burdensome task of caring for their own children, and to assure themselves a life of leisure would delegate to one of the negro slave women the care of their own children.

Many of the upper class white children were cared for by these faithful black "Mammies" fed by the milk from their breasts. Countless stories are told of the love and devotion of the black "Mammy" for the white child who was brought to their 'grown up' years by her care.

A marriage between negroes, before freedom, had no legal standing; a negro couple, wishing to marry, had to get a permit from each master and were united in marriage by a ceremony with a preacher of their own race officiating. After the war, when they were made citizens with civil rights, many former slaves who had been married in this way, hastened to legalize their union by obtaining licenses and having a legal ceremony performed.

While the four years of Civil War, between the North and South resulted in the freedom of the slaves, the negro is yet restricted in many ways in the south. In many states, separate schools are maintained, the negro churches are separate, social equality is not recognized.

In Kentucky, intermarriages between the races are not allowed. Separate coaches are provided on railway trains, hotels, restaurants, theaters and other places of amusement, which cater to white customers, do not permit negro patrons. Many towns and cities have zoning ordinances forbidding negroes to live in white localities. In many southern states the negroes is prevented from voting by local regulations, in Boyd County colored people go to the polls and vote just like anyone else.

Negroes make good house servants, and are extensively used for that purpose today. White families employ them as chauffeurs, butlers, house boys, child nurses, maids and cooks, preferring them to white servants who are not so adaptable to such subordinate positions in life.

Colored men work in barber shops, in restaurants as waiters, and are largely employed as porters in hotels and on railway coaches. Colored women work in hotels as cooks, chamber maids, and are commonly employed as elevator operator in hotels and office buildings.

Not many negroes are in business locally, as race prejudice prevents white folks from trading at colored stores, and the local colored population is too small to provide many customers of their own race. Many ambitious colored folks have left here and gone to the large cities of the north, and made conspicious successes in business. Some have succeeded in the professions as doctors, lawyers, actors, and writers and other vocations.

All in all, the race has progressed to an astonishing degree since being set free a generation ago.

Politics: Formerly, the negro, attributing his freedom to the efforts of Abraham Lincoln in his behalf, voted almost solidly for the Republican Party. Now, however, the Democrats have, by remembering the race when passing out jobs, gained recruits among the colored people, and some negro Democrats are found here. The negro has been accused of voting for money, but it is doubtful if as a race, he is any more prone to this practice than his white fellow citizens among whom this abuse seems to be growing.

BELL CO.
(NELLE SHUMATE)

MANDY GIBSON:

MANDY GIBSON

There were auction-blocks near the court houses where the slaves were sold to the highest bidders. A slave would be placed on a platform and his merits as a speciman of human power and ability to work was enomerated the bidding began. Young slave girls brought high prices because the more slave children that were born on one's plantation the richer he would be in the future. Some slaves were kept just for this purpose, the same as prize thorough-bred stock is kept. In many instances slaves were treated like brutes and their places to sleep were like barn sheds with only a little straw, on which to sleep. Mrs. Neikirk's mother said that she distinctly remembered that the slaves she knew of had only the roughest of food such as: corn bread molasses, and scraps from their owner's table. Their clothing was such as their owners saw fit to give them and the cheapest.

An old negro woman, Aunt Mandy Gibson by name, died last month, Sep. in Middlesboro and I have heard her tell about coming here from Alabama when the town of

Middlesboro was first founded. When asked about her old home people she would go to great lengths to explain about her people having been slaves, but she would always add that they did not mind slavery as they at that time knew nothing of the outdoor life and therefore desired nothing better. She also said that the family that owned her was a kind nature and was good to slaves.

Some of the citizens of Middlesboro today can recall stories that their parents told them about the days when slaves were bought and sold in the United States. Among these is one Mrs. Martha Neikirk, a daughter of an old Union soldier now deceased. Mrs. Rhuben Gilbert, Mrs. Neikirk's mother said that: "Once my mother and I were out in the woods picking huckle-berries and heard a noise as of someone moaning in pain. We kept going toward the sound and finally came to a little brook. Near the water was a negro woman with her head bent over to the ground and weeping as if her heart was broken. Upon asking her what had caused her agony she finally managed to control her emotions enough to sob out her story. The negro woman said then that her master had just sold her to a man that was to take her far away from her present owner and incidently her children. She said this couldn't be helped but she could ask the good Lord to let her die and get out of the misery she was in.

It seems that such incidents were common in those days. Mrs. Sarah Sloan, now residing in Middlesboro tells the stories her mother has told her and she remembers one story in particular about old Aunt Suzy, an old negro slave who, after the close of the Civil War lived near Mrs. Sloan's mother. Aunt Suzy was the property of the Southern plantation owner and had lived on this plantation until she had raised a large family. One day a northern buyer came there and said he wanted to buy some slaves as cheap as possible so, aunt Suzy was getting old and not able to work as she once had, her owner naturally thought that while he had the chance he should sell her but he wanted to keep her children as they were young and able to do hard work. So poor old Aunt Suzy was sold along with some others and taken North. Here she was bought by another trader and sold to a new master. It seems this new master was kind to her and felt sympathy for her in her distress. She told him how she had lived on the old plantation so long and how she had never thought that when she became old and lonely that she would forever be separated from her children so the new [TR: owner?] said he would see what he could do, if anything. He made a trip to her former home and had a talk with the owner of the plantation. The plantation owner said that he had a bad crop year and heavy losses and much as he needed all the help possible to put in more crops he could not afford to buy more slaves, much less one that was unable to work. At this, Aunt Suzy's new owner being a generous, kind-hearted man, decided to give the old lady back to him. He knew he could not get much money for her if he did sell her, for no one wanted an old slave that was unable to work. Aunt Suzy after all her traveling got to return to her old plantation and when the slaves were freed she lived with one of her children until her death.

United States. Work Projects Administration

BREATHITT CO.
(MARGARET BISHOP)

AS TOLD BY SCOTT MITCHELL, A FORMER SLAVE:

SCOTT MITCHELL

Scott Mitchell, claims his age as somewhere in the 70's but his wool is white on the top of his head. Negroes don't whiten near as quickly as white people, evidently he is nearly 90, or there-a-bouts.

"Yes'm I 'members the Civil Wah, 'cause I wuz a-livin' in Christian County whah I wuz bohn, right wif my masteh and mistress. Captin Hester and his wife. I wuz raised on a fahm right wif the, then I lef there.

"Yes, Cap'n Hester traded my mother an my sister, 'Twuz in 1861, he sent em tuh Mississippi. When they wuz 'way from him 'bout two years he bot em back. Yes, he wuz good tuh us. I wuz my mistess' boy. I looked afteh her, en she made all uv my cloes, en she knit my socks, 'cause I wuz her niggah.

"Yes, I wuz twenty yeahs old when I wuz married. I members when I wuz a boy when they had thet Civil Wah. I members theah wuz a brick office wheah they took en hung colohed folks. Yes, the blood wuz a-streamin' down. Sumtimes theah hung them by theah feet, sometimes they hung them by theah thumbs.

"I cum tu Kentucky coal mines when I wuz 'bout twenty years old. I worked for Mistah Jenkins. I worked right here et the Davis, the R.T. Davis coal mine, en at the Bailey mine; that was a-fore Mistah Bailey died.

"When I worked for Mistah Davis he provided a house in the Cutt-Off, that's ovah wheath the mine's at. We woaked frum 7 o'clock in the mawnin' til 6 'clock at night. Yes, I sure liked tuh woak for Mistah Davis. I tended fuahnaces some, too. I sure wuz sorry wen Mistah Davis died."

UNION CO.
(RUBY J. GIRTEN)

A BILL OF SALE:

A BILL OF SALE

This indenture, made and entered into this 5th day of June 1850, by and between Joseph W. Cromwell and Martha Cromwell, his wife, of the first part, and Wm. C. Hamner of the second part, all of the County of Union and State of Kentucky, Witnesseth: That the said Joseph W. Cromwell and Martha his wife, for, and in consideration of the sum of $550.00, in hand paid, the receipt of which is hereby acknowledged, have given, granted, bargained and sold and by these present to grant bargain, sell and deliver unto the said Wm. C. Hamner a certain negro woman called Milly, about 29 years old, and her child, called James, about 18 months old which negroes together with their increase, and the said Joseph W. Cromwell and Martha Cromwell for themselves, their heirs and assigns, will, warrant, and defend unto the said Wm. C. Hamner, his heirs and assigns forever, against the claims of themselves, their heirs, and against the claims of all and every person or persons whatever. Said Cromwell and wife further warrant said negro woman, Milly, to be sound and healthy, and slaves for life. In testimony whereof, the said Joseph W. Cromwell and Martha Cromwell, his wife, have hereunto set the hands and affixed their seals, the day and date first written.

JOSEPH W. CROMWELL
MARTHA L. CROMWELL
WILL—Nancy Austin:

NANCY AUSTIN

In the name of God, Amen. I, Nancy Austin of sound mind and disposing memory, but weak in body, do make and publish this as my last will and Testament.

In the first place I give to my Grandsons, Fielding Jones and Isaac Vanmeter Jones, a negro girl of the name of Margaritte, and negro boy by the name of Solomon to be equally divided between them when the arrive at the age of 21 years or without lawful issue, then and in that case my will and desire is that the survivor have the aforesaid negroes with their increase and should both die without lawful issue, then and that case my will and desire is that the aforesaid negroes and their increase go to my three children and their lawful heirs.

Secondly, I give to my daughter, Harriet Lapham, a negro girl of the name of Mahala, and a boy of the name of Washington, and girl of the name Julian.

Thirdly, I give to my son, Daniel Vanmeter, a negro boy of the name of Alexander, and a negro woman of the name of Teresa, and the horses he claims being 3 in number, and 3 steers, and the hogs he claims, and one bed and furniture.

Fourthly: I give to my daughter, Helen Jones, a negro girl of the name of Sarah, and a boy of the name of John, and a girl of the name of Amanda, and two of the choice of my cows, and one bed a furniture.

Fifthly: My will and desire is that the house and lot I now live on be sold on a 12 months credit with my personal property not heretofore disposed of by my Executor hereafter named or such of them as may qualify, and such as qualify are hereby authorized to convey said house and lot whenever the purchase money is paid to the prchaser[TR: sic] of said house and lot.

Sixthly: My will and desire is that all my just debts be paid and then the balance of the money arising from the sale to be equally divided between my three children and my 2 grandsons, Fielding and Isaac, they taking one fourth of the money between them.

Seventhly: My will and desire is that my faithful servants, Amanda, be free at my death and if she should not be able to support herself then out of the hire or services of the negroes I have given to them. Lastly, I appoint Samuel Casey, Gibson B. Taylor and William Grundy executors of this my last will and Testament as witness my hand this 26th day of May, 1837.

Nancy Austin

Witness: Nathaniel Ashby, C.C. Jones, Tabitha Wilson.

(Will Book B., P.9, at Morganfield, Kentucky.)

ROCKCASTLE CO.
(ROBERT MULLINS)

ROBERT MULLINS

The years 1843 to 1845 worked the development of the systematic enticing away, or stealing of slaves from Kentucky slave owners, and the passing them to Canada by a cordon of posts, or relays, which came to be known as the "Underground Railroad". A number were stolen and carried away on horses. The abductors traveled with the slaves at night and concealed them during the day. The old McFerron house in Mt. Vernon, Kentucky was used as a relay post to hide slaves enroute to Ohio, Michigan and Canada. The slaves in these parts were locked in the old McFerron cellar which was situated under the ground, and they were concealed under the cover until night, when they would travel again.

There were never at any time any slaves sold from auction blocks in this county. It is reported that the life of the slave in Rockcastle County was a happy lot. Their masters built them cabins to live in, furnished with bunks, tables, stoves, and other necessities. Their masters gave them chickens, cows and other stock and gave them plenty to eat.

There are no slaves living in Rockcastle at this time.

United States. Work Projects Administration

CLARK CO.
(MAYME NUNNELLEY)

MAYME NUNNELLEY

The first records of Slaves in Clark County was given by a descendant of one of the members of the little band of resolute Revolutionary soldiers who had been comrades and mess mates throughout the long bloody war. These fifteen families, some from Virginia and others from Maryland, started westward in the early spring of 1783 for Kentucky. They bought with them some horses, a few cattle, thirty or forty slaves and a few necessary household articles.

After many hardships and trials, borne heroically by both men and women, they halted on the banks of the Big Stoner, in what is now the eastern part of Clark County. Two years later another group of families with their slaves came to join this little settlement.

In some cases the owners were good to their slaves had comfortable quarters for them at a reasonable distance from the main house. Their clothing was given them as they needed it. In most instances the clothing was made on the plantation Material woven, and shoes made. The cabins were one and two rooms, maybe more if the families were large. The slaves ate their meals in the kitchen of the main house.

A cruel and inhuman master was ostrazied and taught by the silent contempt of his neighbors a lesson which he seldom failed to learn. In 1789 the general assembly passed an act in which good treatment was enjoined upon master and all contracts between master and slaves were forbidden. The execution of this law was within the jurisdiction of the county courts which were directed to admonish the master of any ill treatment of his slave. If presisted in the court had option and power to declare free the abused slave.

Few traders came to Clark County as the slaves were not sold unless they were unruly. There was no underground railroads through this area.

Among some of the old wills compiled by Dr. George F. Doyle of Winchester, we find wills as follows:

"John Briston in his will dated April 27, 1840 frees his negroes, the executor to go to Todd County and buy land and divide it between the negroes and they were given a cow, three horses and he expressed a desire for them to go to Liberia. They were to be given a certain amount to defray their moving expenses, and buy them provisions and each negro was given his blanket."

"Henry Calmes, in his will dated 1831, divides his slaves among his wife and children." (B7—p654)

"John Christy in his will 1848 says at the death of his wife all his land and slaves are to be sold and the proceeds divided among his children." (B11—p346).

"In some old wills enough slaves are to be sold said all outstanding debts paid and those left to be divided among his heirs."

"A will dated 1837 says at the expiration of eight years after his death all negroes above those bequeated are to be offered to the Colonization Society, if they are of age, to be transported to Liberia and those not of age to continue to serve the persons to whom they are allotted until they come of age, boys 21 and the girls at 18 when they are to be offered to the Colonization Society to be transported to Liberia. None of them are to be forced to go. Those that do not go to Liberia are to continue to serve the persons to whom they are allotted until they are willing to go. Three persons by name to be hired out the seventh year after the death and the money arising from said hire to be given to those that first go to Liberia, $10.00 a piece if there should be so much and the balance given to the next ones to go."

"In the will of Robert Lewis, February 20, 1799, he sets three of his slaves free and gives them the use of 200 acres of the northwest of the Ohio, their life time. There were to be five hired out until their hire amounts to 120 pounds each, then they were to be freed. As the other younger slaves become of age, they are to be freed."

From the following will dated June 22, 1840 it shows the slaves were able, to accumalate an estate:

Allan, Charles   June 22, 1840   Oct 26, 1840

"A free man of color. Estate to be sold and the proceeds distributed as follows: To Ester Graves, a woman of color belonging to the heirs of Rice Arnold, $100.00; balance of money to be divided equally between the children 'I claim to be mine'. Jerrett, Charles, Ester, Carolina, Granvill and Emile; all children of aforesaid. Charlotte Arnold and all belonging to the heirs of Rice Arnold and also Sally, Alfred, Mary, Lucy, Hulda, Catharine, and Maud, children of Ester Graves aforesaid, slaves of Bengamine Graves; also two children of Mary Allan, a slave belonging to Patsey Allan names Lesa and Carolina, the sixteen children to receive an equal share of the money arising from the sale of his estate."

Clark County did not have an auction block or slave market but every New Years day in front of the Courthouse owners would bring their slaves to be hired. It was told by one of the old citizens a few years ago, (died two years ago) that he walked nine miles one bitter cold day to hire some slaves. These could be hired for a definite time or until they brought certain amounts of money.

In 1812-1814 Winchester, the County Seat of Clark County boasted of a weekly newspaper, issued every Saturday. From the advertisement column of this paper we learned that Dillard Collins was willing to pay $10.00 to get his run away slave, Reuben, and a similar reward was offered for one "Scipio" who had taken French leave from his master, (donned) in his master's new clothes. Another ad in this paper ways[TR: says?] one Walter Karrick offered to trade a negro woman for "whiskey", cyder and flour.

"A story is told of a slave "Monk Estill" who helped or rather belonged to Col. James Estill of Madison County. In 1782 in a battle known as Estill's defeat, which occured on the grounds where Mt. Sterling now stands in

Montgomery County, Col. Estill and twenty-five men attacked a party of Wyandotte Indians by whom the slave was taken prisoner.

"In the thickest of the fight, Monk called out in a loud voice; 'Don't give way, Marse Jim, there's only twenty-five Indians and you con whip all of them.'

"Col. Estill was killed and the men retreated. Monk escaped from his captors and after many hardships joined the white comrades.

"On his shoulder he carried a wounded soldier twenty-five miles to Estill Station. His young master gave him his freedom in recognition for his bravery and supported him in comfort the rest of his life."

In Clark County are many small negroe settlements formed by the old freed slaves after the war. Some had accumalated a little and brought a small piece of land and others had homes given to them by their owners.

Mr. Archilles Eubank was the largest slave holder of his day, Mr. Colby Quisenberry was second, in Clarks County.

"The story is told that at the time of General Morgan's last raid on Winchester, an old faithful slave of Dr. Hubbard Taylor, (a noted Physician all over this portion of Kentucky at this time) who was always careful of his master's interests, and without the consent of his master, saved his very fine riding horse, "Black Prince" from being pressed into service of the Confederates. Ab (the slaves name) learned that Morgan's men were good judges of horse flesh and had taken several horses just as the Federals did when they needed them and he determined to conceal prince, whose groom he was. He put him there in the smoke house along with the meat, but Prince pawed and made disturbances until he took him out and took him to the cellar persuading him to descend the steps and left him there. He came up to hear that several horses had been taken from the cellars of the men, then he hastened back to get Black Prince. He brought him out of the cellar and took him to the Laundry room and sat there with him conversing him to keep him quite until all danger passed. When Prince became restless and wanted to paw his way out, old Ab would say, "Now Prince, you quit dat you's in danger of being taken by the bad soldiers." Old Prince would stop instantly and listen to his groom."

MONTGOMERY CO.
(GLADYS ROBERTSON)

GLADYS ROBERTSON

In this community most of the slaves were kept on farms and each family was given a well constructed log house. They were fed by provisions given them by their white masters and they were plentiful. They were clothed by their masters. These clothes were made by the colored women under the direction and supervision of their mistress, the white woman cut the clothes for both men and women, and the colored women did the sewing of the garments. The men did the manual labor on the farm and the women the domestic. Each white woman and girl had a special servant for her own use and care and each white man had his colored man or valet.

There are no records of a big slave trade in this county. When a slave was sold it was usually to a friend or neighbor and most masters were very considerate and would not sell unless a family could go together. For instance from the diary of Mrs. Wliza[TR: Eliza?] Magowan 1853-1871, we read this: "Lina and two children Scott and Dulcina sold to J. Wilkerson". Also another item: "Violet married to Dennie" showing that care was taken that marriages were made among the negroes.

The darkies had suppers in their own quarters and had much merrymaking and laughter.

Illness among the darkies were cared from among themselves but under the watchful eye of the master and mistress.

The darkies were deeply religious and learned much of the Bible from devout mistresses who felt it their holy duty to teach these ignorant people the word of God. An extract from Mrs. Magowan's diary on July 25, 1856: "Old Aunt Becky was baptised on the 20th; she being upwards of 70 years of age. A considerable interest on the subject of religion is manifest among the negroes, several have joined may they be kept by the power of God unto Salvation. The redemption of the soul is precious". This is quoted to show that the Negro was considered as a human being and treated as such.

Also taken from Mrs. Magowan's diary: "Dove sold to Mr. Van Thompson. O slavery, thorn art a bitter draught! tho' thousands have tasted of thee, thou art none the less bitter."

The Underground Railroad did not run through this county. No slaves were carried away on any such thing. The older people interviewed about this say they do not believe such a railroad ever existed as it would be a feat of engineering even in this day and time.

The rosters of the Independent company which Ge. John S. Williams organized in this county and led to Mexico is in the possession of his grandson Mr. John S.W. Hollaway, Winchester, Kentucky.

Mrs. Allie R. Robertson has in her possession the suit

worn home from the war, by her father Joe Arrasmith. He was in the company of Morgan's men. It is made of coarse cotton and was in a most deplorable condition when he came home.

United States. Work Projects Administration

MONROE CO.
(LENNETH JONES)

(UNCLE) EDD SHIRLEY:

EDD SHIRLEY

I am 97 years and my name is Uncle Edd Shirley and I am still working as janitor and support my family. My father was a white man and my mother was a colored lady. I was owned three different times, or rather was sold to three different families. I was first owned by the Waldens; then I was sold to a man by the name of Jackson, of Glasgow, Kentucky. Then my father, of this county, bought me.

I have had many slave experiences. Some slaves were treated good, and some were treated awful bad by the white people; but most of them were treated good if they would do what their master told them to do.

I onced saw a light colored gal tied to the rafters of a barn, and her master whipped her until blood ran down her back and made a large pool on the ground. And I have seen negro men tied to stakes drove in the ground and whipped because they would not mind their master; but most white folks were better to their slaves and treated them better than they are now. After their work in the fields was finished on Saturday, they would have parties and have a good time. Some old negro man would play the banjo while the young darkies would dance and sing. The white folks would set around and watch; and would sometimes join in and dance and sing.

My colored grandfather lived to be 115 years old, and at that age he was never sick in his life. One day he picked up the water bucket to go to the spring, and as he was on his way back he dropped dead.

The Story of Mrs. C. Hood:

Once upon a time during the Civil War my grandmother was alone with just one old faithful servant. The Union troops had just about taken everything she had, except three prize saddle horses and one coal black mare which she rode all the time. She was very fond of the mare and valued it very much. One night my grandmother heard a noise, and called old Joe to go to the barn and see what was the matter. As he was nearing the barn someone yelled "Halt"; and Joe being a black man and a servant, stopped just where he was. My grandmother, who had also heard the command, paid no attention whatsoever; she went straight through the dozen or more Union soldiers who were stealing her stock to the one who appeared to be the leader. He was holding her mare; she jerked the briddle from his hand, led her mare back to the kitchen door, where she held her the remainder of the night.

A Story:

When my mother was a girl she was staying with some kinfolks for one month. These people owned several slaves and among them was one old man-servant who was very old and had served out his usefulness. It was war time and food was scarce even for the white folks. The younger and stronger slaves got most of the food, and old Tom was always hungry. My mother finding this out, and feeling sorry for him would slip him bread and other food through a hole in the kitchen floor. A short time after this, my mother married and moved to a home of her own. Old Tom never forgot her kindness; and finally persuaded his master to give him to my mother, who kept him until his death.

United States. Work Projects Administration

ESTILL CO.
(EVELYN MCLEMORE)

STORY OF PETER BRUNER, A FORMER SLAVE:

PETER BRUNER

Peter Bruner, was born in Winchester, Kentucky, Clark Co., in 1845. His master was John Bell Bruner, who at that time treated him fairly well. When Peter was 10 years of age his master brought him and his sister to Irvine. After arriving in Irvine, Peter's master was very cruel to him. They got only cornbread, fat meat and water to eat. If his master's hunger was not satisfied, he would even take this little from them. The[TR:?] were tables to eat from.

Once Peter, was taken into his master's house to nurse the children and was made to sleep on the floor with only a ragged quilt to lie on and one thin one over him.

Often he was whipped because his mistress said the washing was not clean, when it was. On one occasion when he was beaten his master took a piece of sole leather about 1 foot long and 2 inches wide, cut it full of holes and dipped it in water that was brined. He then took the leather and lashed the poor slave's back.

Joe Bruner, was a better master to his slaves than John. Once when Peter stole some sugar and flour, that he and his sister might have a pound cake, Joe caught him. He did not whip him however, because he knew that Peter did not often have enough to eat.

Peter, endured torture as long as he could and finally decided to escape. He went to Richmond, Kentucky on to Lexington. On his way he made a contract with a man to drive his horses to Orleans, but was caught while in Lexington. On his way they caught him and took him to jail and he remained until his master came for him. This did not down him, for just as soon as he could he escaped again, and this time got as far as Xenia, Ohio, but was again caught and brought back. This time he was severely beaten for three hours.

When 17 years old, Peter was hired out to Jimmy Benton, who was more cruel than John Bruner, but was again brought back. It was then that he tried again to escape. This time he went through Madison Co. near Sugar Creek. This was about the year 1861, when the war had begun. Again he was caught and taken back, but this time by Joe Bruner. He escaped several times, but never could seem to get anywhere. Once when he and another slave, Phil, escaped they were caught and made to walk the entire distance barefoot. After this Peter, was chained each night to a chair. One morning while eating his breakfast he heard a knock at the door and on opening it he found a troop of Union Home Guards. Jim Benton and John Bruner were taken to prison. After this Peter went to Miller's Creek and worked at odd jobs for awhile.

When John Bruner was taken from Prison, he was much better to Peter. Soon after John was released from Prison,

Peter escaped again. This time he had joined a regiment in the war. He went through hardships, cold, hunger and illness.

Often when they were awaken in the morning they would find their blankets frozen to the ground. He was sick several times. His feet frozen and other things would go wrong such as having fever and once he had Variloid. After serving for awhile he was mustered out and returned to Winchester, where his mother lived. He stayed a short time and then went to Oxford, Ohio. Here he went to school, but soon decided he was not learning anything so decided to get married. In the spring he was married to Nannie Proctor. Again he made a mistake and during this time suffered hardships trying to keep a roof over their heads and food enough to eat. He worked at odd jobs, but could not find much to do and got very much in debt. He then went to Hamilton, Ohio and asked Mr. John Frye to loan him some money. He had asked Mr. Roberts for some and he would not loan it. However, John Frye did loan him the money and Peter paid himself out of debt and bought a stone quarry from his mother-in-law. He sold a lot of stone from it, but finally sold this and took a job as engineer at Oxford, College. Dr. Walker was president at that time. It was here that Peter celebrated his 25th wedding anniversary. The teacher, faculty and seniors made this a happy day for him. He got a job as janitor under Dr. Thompson at Miami University. He worked here for 13 years under President Taft. He is a member of Bethel A.M.E. Church and has been for over 50 years. In 1918 he and his wife celebrated his golden anniversary.

Peter Bruner is still living (1936) but his eyesight is impaired. He is 91 years of age.

United States. Work Projects Administration

CHRISTIAN CO.
(MAMIE HANBERY) [HW: KY 3]

STORY OF EASTER SUDIE CAMPBELL,
(AGE ABOUT 72, WEBBER ST., HOPKINSVILLE, KY.)

EASTER SUDIE CAMPBELL

Born in Princeton, Caldwell Co., Kentucky, her parents were slaves, the property of Will and Martha Grooms of Princeton.

Aunt Easter as she is called has followed the profession of a mid-wife for forty years. She is still active and works at present among the negroes of Hopkinsville.

"Yes, sho, I make my own medicines, humph, dat aint no trouble. I cans cure scrofula wid burdock root and one half spoon of citrate of potash. Jes make a tea of burdock root en add the citrate of potash to hit. Sasafras is good foh de stomach en cleans yer out good. I'se uses yeller percoon root foh de sore eyes.

"Wen I stayed wid Mrs. Porter her chaps would break out mighty bad wid sores in de fall of de year and I'se told Mrs. Porter I'se could core dat so I'se got me some elder berries en made pies out of hit en made her chaps eat hit on dey war soon cored.

"If twont foh de white folks I sho would hev a hard time. My man he jes wen erway en I haint neber seed him ergin en I'se had five chilluns en de white folks hev heped me all dese years. Dese trifling niggers dey wont hepe dey own kind of folks. If youse got de tooth ache I makes a poultice of scrape irish pertatoes en puts hit on de jaw on de side de tooth is aching en dat sho takes de fever out of de tooth. I'se blows terbacco smoke in de ear en dat stops de ear ache.

"Wen I goes on er baby case I jest let nature hev hits way. I'se alays teas de baby de first thing I does is ter blow my breath in de baby's muff en I spanks it jes a little so hit will cry den I gives hit warm catnip tea so if hit is gwine ter hev de hives dey will break out on hit. I alays hev my own catnip en sheep balls foh sum cases need one kind of tea en sum ernother. I give sink field tea ter foh de colic. Hit is jes good fuh young baby's stomach. I'se been granning foh nigh unter forty year en I'se only lost two babies, dat war born erlive. One of dese war de white man's fault, dis baby war born wid de jaundice en I tolds dis white man ter go ter de store en git me sum calomel en he says, "whoeber heard of givin a baby sech truck", an so dat baby died.

"Of course youse can tell wheder the baby is gwine ter be a boy er girl fore tis born. If de mother carries dat child more on de left en high up dat baby will be a boy en if she carries hit more ter de middle dat will be a girl. Mothers oughter be more careful while carrying dar chilluns not ter git scared of enthing foh dey will sho mark dar babies wid turrible ugly things. I knows once a young wooman war expecting en she goes black-berry hunting en er bull cow wid long horns got after her en she was so scairt dat she threw her hands ober her head en wen dat baby boy war born he hed to nubs on his head jes like horns beginning ter grow so I'se hed her call her doctor en dey cuts dem off. One white wooman I'se waited on like hot choclate en she alays wanted more she neber hed nuff of dat stuff en one day she spills sum on her laig en it jes splotched en burned her en wen dat gal war born she hed a big brown spot on her laig jes like her Mammy's scar frum de burn. Now you see I noes yer ken mark de babies.

"Dar war a colored wooman once I'se waited on dat hed to help de white folks kill hogs en she neber did like hog liver but de white folks told her ter take one home en fix hit foh her supper. Well she picked dat thing up en started off wid hit en hit made her feel creepy all ober en dat night her baby war born a gal child en de print of er big hog-liver war standing out all ober one side of her face. Dat side of her face is all blue er purplish en jes the shape of a liver. En hits still dar.

"I'se grannied ober three hundred chilluns en I noes wat I'se talking about.

"Hee! Hee! Hee! One day dar war a circus in Hopkinsville en er black wooman I'se war ergoing ter wait on war on de street to watch foh de parade en wid de bands er playing en de wild varmits en things dis woman give birth ter dat girl chile on de corner of Webber and Seventh St. Dat gal sho got er funny name 'Es-pe-cu-liar'. (I did not get the drift of the story so I asked her what was so funny about the name. Of course it is a name I have never heard before so the following is what the girls Mother said about it to Aunt Easter. M.D. Hanbery)

"Well the gals Mammy thought hit war jes peculiar dat, dat happened wen she war er looking at the parade. (So this woman Especuliar is still in Hopkinsville and her story is known in quite a few of the older circles.)

"Yah! Yah! I sho remember how de ole folks uster dress. De women wore hop skirts en de men wore tight breeches. De night gowns war made on er yoke aufull full en big long sleeves wid a cuff at de hand en a deep hem at de bottom of de gown, dese gowns war made of domestic en wen dey war washed en starched en ironed dey wur be so stiff dey could stand erlone." De men en de women both wore night caps. If de gown war a dress up gown why dey war home made knit en crochet lace in de front en lots en lots of tucks some of dem had deep ruffles on dem at the bottom.

"Wen my Pappy kum home from de war, he war on de "Govmint" side he brung a pistol back wid him dat shot a ball dey hed caps on hit en used dese in de war. De Ku Klux jum after him one night en he got three of dem wid dis pistol, nobody eber knowed who got dose Kluxes.

Ghosts— —

"Sho dar is ghosts. One night es I war going home from work de tallest man I eber seed followed me wid de prettiest white shirt on en den he passed me, en waited at de corner I war a feeling creepy en wanter run but jes couldn't git my laigs ter move en wen I'se git ter de corner war he war I said 'Good Ebening' en I seed him plain es day en de did not speak en jes disappeared right fore my eyes.

"Den ergin I went ter de fish pond one day fishing en

cotched two or three big fish wen I went home thot I'd go back dat night en I begun to dig sum fishing worms en my boss he saw me en axed, 'Wot I doing'. I told him I war ergoing ter de pond ter fish dat night. He said 'don you go ter dat pond ternight Easter foh if you does something will run you erway.' I jes laughed at him en dat night I en my boy wese goes ter de pond en as we war er standing in dar quiet like we heared something squeeching like er new saddle en er horses er trotting. We listened en waited wen something wen inter dat pond right twixt us liker er ball er fire. Weums sho did leave dar an de next morning my boss axed me if we cotched enthing en we told him wot we saw en he said he knowed weums would be run erway foh he war run erway hisself.

"Course dar is hainted houses dese haints in dese places jes wont leave you erlone. Wen I'se war er living in Princeton, Uncle Lige my Mammy's brother en I'se moved in er cabin one Christmas day en war ergoing ter stay dar en dat night we war er setting bore de fire en de fire light war es bright as day, wen I looks up at de wall foh I hears er scratching noise en dar war er big white cat on de wall wid all he's hair standing on dat cat jos jumps from wall ter de nother en Uncle Lige en me jes open dat cabin door en started ter de tother cabins on de place en we deed dat thing dat war bigger den eny cat I eber seed jes come thru dat door in de air en hit de front gate, dis gate hed er iron weight on hit so hit would stay shot en dis thing hit at de top den wen erway. No I neber seed whar hit went. Dis gate jes banged en banged all night. We could heat from de tother cabin. Uncle Liga en me moved erway next day en other people moved in dis cabin en dey saw de same thing en nobody would stay dar. Dem some time after dis diz cabin war torn down.

"Once I hed a dream I knowed I ner bout saw hit. I alays did cook ebery night er pot er beans on de fire foh de chilluns ter eat next day while I war at work en Lizzie my daughter uster git up in de night en git her some beans en eat dem en dis dream war so real dat I couldn't tell if hit war Lizzie er no but dis wooman jes glided by my bed en went afore de fire en stood dar den she jes went twixt my bed en went by de wall. I jes knowed wen I woke up dat my child was sick dat lived erway from home en wanted my son ter take me ter see her. He said he would go hisself en see so he wen en wen he come back he hed a headache en fore morning dat nigger war dead. So you see dat war de sign of da dream. I war jes warned in de dream en didn't hev sense nuff ter know hit."

[STORY OF UNCLE DICK:]

UNCLE DICK

Uncle Dick, a negro servant of one of the Hendersons, was the fiddler of the neighborhood at weddings, husking parties and dances. Dick's presence was essential. Uncle Dick was fully aware of his own importance, and in consequence assumed a great deal of dignity in his bearing. Before setting out he always dressed himself with the greatest nicety. At the appointed time he was at the place with all the weight of his dignity upon him. Woe to the "darkies" who violated any of the laws of etiquette in his presence.

On a certain evening there was to be a grand wedding festival among the colored gentry on a farm about 6 miles from Uncle Dick's residence. He was, of course called upon to officiate as master of ceremonies. He donned his long-tailed blue coat, having carefully polished the glittering gilt buttons; then raised his immense shirt collar, which he considered essential to his dignity, and, fiddle in hand, sallied forth alone. The younger folk had set out sometime before; but Uncle Dick was not to be hurried out of his dignity.

The narrow path led, for the greater part of the way, through a dense forest, which was as wild as when roamed by the Indians. A heavy snow lay on the ground, on which the moonbeams were shining whenever they could force a passage through the trees.

The dreary solitude of the way made no impression on the mind of Uncle Dick. He was anxiously hurrying on to reach the scene of operation, having spent a little too much time in polishing his gilt buttons.

On he dashed, heedless of the black shadows and hideous night cries of the deep forest. Wolves were howling around him; but he paid no attention to sounds so common, thinking only of the feet that were waiting his arrival to be set in motion.

Soon, however, the howling began to approach nearer than was agreeable, The wolves continued to become more and more noisy, till, to his indescribable horror, he heard them on each side of the crackling bushes.

Very soon the woods seemed to the old man to be alive with the yelling pack. Wolves are cautious about attacking human beings; they usually require some little time to work themselves up to the point. Every few moments a dark object would brush past poor old Dick's legs with a snapping sound like that of a steel trap, while the yelling and crackling increased with terrible rapidity.

Dick new that to run would mean instant death, as the cowardly pack would all rush on him the moment he showed fear. His only chance of safety consisted in preserving the utmost coolness. A short distance before him lay some open ground; and he hoped that on reaching this they would leave him, as they do not like to make an attack in such a place.

He remembered, too, that in the middle of the open space there stood an old cabin, in which he might be able to find refuge. But now the wolves rushed at him more and more boldly, snapping in closer and closer proximity to his legs.

Snap! Snap! Nearer and nearer! Instinctively he thrust out his fiddle at them. The jarring of the strings made than leap back. Hope returned. He drew his hand violently across the strings—twang, twang! Instantly the wolves sprang back as if he had fired a gun among them.

He was now at the edge of the open space. He twanged his fiddle—the wolves recoiled. Dick rushed toward the hut with all his speed, raking the strings more violently at every jump, till they rang again.

The astonished wolves paused for a moment on the edge of the open ground, with tails between their legs. But the sight of his flying form renewed their savage instincts. With a loud burst of yells they darted after him at full speed. He reached the hut just as the jaws of the foremost wolf opened to seize him.

He rushed in, and the closing door dashed against the nose of the nearest beast. The door was too rickety to keep the enemy out; but Dick had time to push himself through the broken roof and get on top of the cabin. The wolves were now furious. Rushing into the hut, they jumped and snapped at him, so that Dick almost felt their teeth. It required the greatest activity to keep his legs out of their reach.

Notwithstanding his agonizing terror, he still clung to his fiffle. Now, in desperation, as he was kicking his feet in the air to avoid their steel like fangs, he drew his bow shrieking across the strings. The yells instantly ceased. Dick continued to make the most frightful spasms of sound, but the wolves could not long endure bad fiddling. As soon as the first surprise was over the attack was renewed more furiously than ever.

A monstrous head was now thrust up between the boards of the roof, only a few inches from Dick. He gave himself up for lost. But the excess of terror seemed to stimulate him, so that almost of their own accord his fingers began to play "Yankee-Doodle." Instantly there was complete silence! The silence continued as long as he continued to play; but the moment he ceased the listeners again became furious, and rushed on with increased ferocity.

Uncle Dick's pride as a fiddler was flattered. He entered for awhile completely into the spirit of the thing. But never before had he played to an audience so fond of music. They permitted no pause. His enthusiasm began to give way to cold and fatigue. He was tired to death and almost frozen.

What was to be done? There sat the listeners with tongues lolling and ears pricked up, allowing not a moments pause, but demanding an uninterrupted stream of music. Several weary hours passed, and Uncle Dick was almost exhausted.

But all this while the wedding company had been anxiously expecting their musician. Becoming at last impatient or alarmed, some of them set out in search for him. They found him on top of the hut, still sawing away for for life. The wolves were driven away and Uncle Dick was relieved from his unwilling efforts to charm listeners who got more music than they paid for.

Last Wolf: [HW: KY4]

On January 20, 1910, a famous gray wolf was seen in Christian County and killed by a man named Tyler. This wolf seemed to be the last wolf seen in this County. It had terrorized the farmers in the Sinking Fork neighborhood, and a party organized by Charles L. Dade formed to hunt and kill this wolf which was done on the above date. The wolf measured 48 inches from tip to tip and stood 24 inches high.

Negro Holiness Meetings:

Once a year a group of 200 or 300 negroes give a religious Camp Meeting in a field on the Canton Pike about one mile southeast of Hopkinsville. There is quite a settlement of negroes call themselves or their church the Holiness Church. They claim to be sanctified and cannot sin. A few nights ago I was invited to attend one of these meetings, the negroes reserve some benches under the tent for white people.

The night that I attended there were two preachers and it seems as though it is the duty of these preachers to bring their discourse to such a point as to play on the emotions of their congregation. The order of service begun with a hymn by the choir. The music for this consisted of a piano, banjo guitar and numerous tambourines. The negroes being naturally born with a great sense of rhythm the songs were not in the same tempo as the songs of the whites but were of a jazz tempo and with the banjo and tambourines it makes one think of the stories of the African jungles. The services start around 7:30 P.M. and usually break up around midnight.

The negroes in about one hour after the services start being[TR: begin?] to testify and then after each testimony someone offers a prayer then by this time someone in the congregation will be worked up to the pitch of shouting "Glory Hallelulah". "When this shout starts the tambourine players will begin shaking the tambourines and shortly the majority of the congregation would be shouting, moaning or praying. The tambourines players bounce around in time to the music. There were some excellent untrained voices, in the choir and the congregation. The mourners bench was always full of mourners and when one of the Mourners would begin to shout the "Workers" would then let the congregation know that this brother or sister had repented by saying "Lets pray for Bro. or Sister ----, for he or she had "Come Through". The congregation would begin clapping their hands while this prayer was in progress and general moanings with one or both of the preachers praying at the same time why this brother or sister is taken in to the flock to sin no more.

While the above is in progress there are other workers talking and singing to the rest of the mourners and when two or three "Come Through" at once there is great shouting rejoicing, clapping of hands and the tambourines continue to clang and the choir members dance and this process continues for hours or until the preachers become so exausted with their exhortations and contortions that the meeting is adjourned.

Superstitions of the Negro Race:

In interviewing the different negroes in this community I have not found a single negro that could admit if I asked the direct question that they are the least bit superstitious. The following story happened in my experience with this race about ten years ago.

Fifteen years ago I purchased a farm from the estate of a gentleman that had committed suicide. It seems as though the gentleman took his gun and told the family that he was going to the tobacco barn to shoot rats. This barn was located a short distance from the main dwelling on the farm and then on the other side of this barn were three negro tenant houses.

My first trouble with negroes superstition was to get a tenant to inhabit the house nearest the barn. This cabin was in better repair and larger than the other two cabins and the hardest thing to do was to get a tenant or negro cropper to take this cabin.

They would give every excuse imaginable but the direct answer until finally one man I was trying to make a trade with admitted that "De cabin war ter clos ter de barn Mr. ---- killed himself in." Finally I prevailed on this man to move in by giving him a different garden spot, hog-pen and cowpen as these were still nearer the barn. In fact I moved those buildings thinking I would have an easier time gettin a tenant the next year.

Everything went along beautifully until time came to House the tobacco and not a negro cropper would use this barn for his tobacco. So I had my individual crop housed in this barn. As the type of tobacco mostly grown at that time was bark fired someone had to stay at the barn night and day to attend the fires and watch that a stick of tobacco did not drop in the blaze and burn the barn and contents. As long as my husband or myself stayed in or around the barn we did not have trouble with these darkies but sometimes it to attend to other matters on this farm and had to leave a hired negro in charge and as soon as we would get out of sight of the barn the negro would desert his post. It became evident that one or the other of us stay at this barn night and day until firing season was over. The same thing happened when the stripping season began. These conditions continued until a wind storm blew this barn down. Still I hoard some of the negroes express their thoughts.

Mr. G- - - - sho had no tention of dat barn standing. I had the tenants separate this lumber for different uses on the farm and the scrap lumber was to be taken to the cabin or the main dwelling to be used as kindling and not a negroe would use this kindling. One negro a tall black man around seventy years old said, "No dat wood wont burn". I asked, "Why"? He said, "Mr. G- - - - would sho hant me if I teched a single piece of dat wood ter burn." So naturally the main dwelling had a bountiful supply of kindling.

This farm was watered by a big spring and branch that ran along behind the stables and near this particular barn and this branch run into a big sink hole and then through a small crevice underground. Once cold and disagreeable winter something blocked this crevice and the waters soon overflowed the sink hole and extended all over the lowlands near. The winter was severely cold and this water began to moderate and a light drizzle of rain was falling and most of the tenants on the farm had retired for the night when suddenly this ice on the stream broke up and in some manner the crevice had been opened and the sound from this water going in its course underground was terrific. My family as well as myself were very much frightened. No one can imagine the commotion that existed at the cabins on the tenant row near the stream. Negroes poured from the cabins in all manners of dress or undress even the cold weather did not tempt them to take time to don shoes and hose but came to the back door of my house some crying and moaning and praying, and if there is such a thing as a pale negro these darkies were certainly pale, eyes rolling and the majority of them wanting to leave the farm before daybreak or by that time anyway or else staying in our home all night. Fires were made in the kitchen and they congregated there and most of them remained there all night. One old negro said or acted as spokesman for the crowd. "Dat all this crowd of niggers need dat Mr. G---- was afer dem and meant foh dem to move or git."

My husband took one or two of the older men with lanterns and made an investigation. When they reached the branch the overflow was gone and there was no evidence that there had been any water over these fields except for the large blocks of ice that was lying in the field.

With much persuading and cajoling the majority of these negroes went to their cabins that night and the most skeptical stayed in my kitchen all the rest of the night. But peace and quiet reigned once more and from that day as long as these tenants remained with me I did not have any trouble with them being superstitious but each time the tenants were changed the same superstitions had to be met with and their fears had to be quieted.

Negro Folk Songs: (Contributed by William Warfield, Col.)

These songs more commonly called plantation melodies, originated with the negroes of the South during the days of slavery. They habe been somewhat collected and written about.

These songs have for the Negro the same value that the folk songs of any people have for that people. In the days of slavery they furnished an outlet for aching hearts and anguished souls. Today they help to foster race pride and to remind the race of the "rock from which it was hewn". Some of these folk songs represented the lighter side of the slave's life, as for example,

> "Heave away! Heave away!
> I'd rudder co't a yallar gal
> Dan work foh Henry Clay
> Heave away, yaller gal, I want to go."

or:

> "Ole Massa take dat new brown coat,
> And hang it on de wall;
> Dat darkey take dat same old coat,
> And wear it to de ball,
> Oh, don't you hear my tru lub sing?"

It was in their religious song, however that they poured out their souls. Three things are especially emphasized in these song. First this life is full of sorrow or trouble:

> "Nobody knows da truble I sees,
> Nobody but Jesus."

Second, religion is the best thing in the world. It enables you, though a slave, to have joy of the soul, to endure the trials. Future life is happy and eternal:

> "We'll walk dem golden streets,
> We'll walk dem golden streets,
> We'll walk dem golden streets,
> Wear pleasure nebber dies."

or:

> "Oh! I'se a-gwine to lib always,
> Oh! I'se a-gwine to lib always,
> Oh! I'se a-gwine to lib always,
> Wen I git in de kingdom."

United States. Work Projects Administration

ANNIE MORGAN:

ANNIE MORGAN

Story of Annie Morgan: (age 65, 207 W. 2nd St., Hopkinsville, Ky.) Annie was born of slave parents. Her mother and father were slaves of the Payne family.

Ques: Annie can you give me or rather tell me of some of your earlier life with your parents, or what your mother and father has told you of things before and after the Civil War.

Ans: Wal, wal, I do declare it has ben so long I'se jes don't remember. I'se seem to remember de big days we uster hav on Proclamation Day wen we used ter go to Grandmums who lived in Trigg County. Foh days befur weuns would git redy ter go in a wagon and as dar was a heap of chilluns it tuk quite a time an weuns would start by day break and dem wen we got dar why all de rest of the daughters en sons of dar chilluns was alredy that, den weun's hev a big time wid watermullins and ebything good to eat. Some times Uncle Ben brot hid bajo and us chilluns would dance.

Ques: Annie did you ever have a dream to come true? Or do you believe in dreams?

Ans: Sho does, sho does, why chile all my dream come true. I recollect one wen my son was sick, I felt he wont gwine to git well. I asked him, "Was he right with God", he says, "Dar is nuthin between me and de Lawd". Den afterwards, I begin to worry gin about dis boy, I prays "De Lawd" and ax him ter let me drem a drem bout him an nite time I did, I could see dis boy jist as plain crossing "Judgment Stream" and I says to him in my drem, I say, "You come my son, he's crossin Judgment Stream, I says ter ole man go in and hep him" and my son says to me, "I'm crossing Judgment Stream, Mammy, and I got to cross it myself". I says "I no you are cold now". I dreamed I spread a rug round him den he disappeared, inter de building, by dat time I woke up so happy. Oh, Lawd, ter no my boy was in Heben. I am sho I would not dremed dat drem unless "De Lawd" tended me ter no my boy was saved. I sho nos dis boy is in Heben.

"Wen me an my man was married all de colored folks in the neighborhood come to ma's and weums my husband and me jumped o'er the broom stick an we was been married, ebery since. In dese days hit were too far ter go git a preacher an most colored folks married dat way."

STORY OF CORA TORIAN: (217 W. 2ND ST., HOPKINSVILLE, KY.—AGE 71.)

CORA TORIAN

Bell Childress, Cora's Mother, was a slave of Andrew Owen. He purchased Belle Childress in the Purchase and brought her to Christian County. Cora was born in Christian County on Mr. Owen's farm and considered herself three years old at the end of the Civil War. She told me as follows:

"I has dreamed of fish and dat is a sure sign dat I would git a piece of money, an I always did. Dreamed of buggy and horse an it was a sign of death in family and I no's hits tru. Dream of de ded hit always rains. My Mistus and Marster fed and clothed us good and we lived in a little log cabin of one room and cooked on an open fire. Some Marsters wud whoop ther slaves til the blood would run down daw backs dese slaves would run away sometimes den sum would come to Ise Marse and would have to send dem back to dar own marsters and how my ole marster hated to see dem go.

"I hang horse shoes oer my door to keep the Evil Spirits away. My Mammy always wore and ole petticoat full gather at de waist band wid long pockets in dem and den to keep peace in de house she would turn de pocket wrong side out jes as she would go to somebodys elses house.

"I sho do no dar is ghosts, I seed one oncet hit was a man wid no head on standin in my house and pullin the crammin out of de house and puttin hit on de table. Oooh I no's dat is so cause I seed hit wid my own eyes.

"My Mammy had a woman dat lived wid us and she died, and sometimes afterwards, she called me and I looked in de room and dis woman was sitting on de side of de bed and wen i spoke to her she slowly ris up and went thru a crack about two inches wide. now dats a fak!

"Humph, no I'se not gwine ter go near no hainted house, much less stay in one. I'se scairt.

"Hee, hee, sho you can find things by spitting in yer han and de way the spit goes if youse will go dar you will be sho to find hit.

"Aint got no time for fortune tellers, don believe in dem, day don't do nuthin.

"Wen de moon changes if youse see hit thru de bresh you sho will have bad luck, but if youse sees hit and nuthin to hinder youse from lookin at hit straight and make a wish it who will come true. I'se no's cause my son was way down South an I woant to seed him and I looks at de moon and hit was changing and I wished de would come home and looked up de road and "Lawd daw he were.

"Youse plants de pertatoes by de moon. Irish pertatoes planted on de light of de moon will go ter vine and der neber will be a tater on de vine. If youse plant dem by de dark of de moon yourall's pertatoes will be plentiful.

"If youse maks soap it must be made by de light of de moon or de soap will all turn to grease.

"If youse sneeze wen you eats you will shorely die.

"If youse see a blue gummed negro be shore one don bite you foh dey are shore pizenous.

"If youse have yer year to ring, sho sing of death.

"Move on Friday, "Good Lawd No", youse would sho have bad luck.

"One tru sign of death, if a dog howls at midnight, you will sho to die. If you dreams of you teeth falling out is a tru sign of death and if youse dreams of a marriage is nuther tru sign of death.

"If I dream of a naked purson I'se is sho to die. No cat mus come in wen dar is a ded body for de cat will sho eat de body.

"If a cat crosses youse path to de left some kind of bad luck is sho to overtake on yer journey.

"If a peckerwood pecks on de roof of youse house you will sho lose some member of youse family. Dey is pizen.

"No I'se jes ter scairt ter go whar day call up Spirits."

United States. Work Projects Administration

TALE OF MARY WOOLDRIDGE: (CLARKSVILLE PIKE—AGE ABOUT 103.)

MARY WOOLDRIDGE

"Mary and her twin sister were slaves born in Washington County, Kentucky, near Lexington, belonging to Bob Eaglin. When Mary was about fourteen years old she and her sister was brought to the Lexington slave market and sold and a Mr. Lewis Burns of the same County purchased her. Mary doesn't know what became of her sister. Five or six years later she was again put on the block and sold to a Negro Trader but Mary does not remember this traders name. While here she was kept in a stockade and it was several years before she again was bought by a white man. Mr. Thomas McElroy near Lexington bought her and she remained his slave until the slaves were freed. Mary looks her age. She is a tall gaunt black Negro with white hair about one inch long and very kinky, and still she dresses as the older slave woman dressed in the past days. She wears an old bodice with a very full skirt that comes to her ankles and this skirt has very long deep pockets and when I asked her why she had such pockets in her skirt her answer was, "Wal you sees honey I jes am used ter dis dress and thar is no way foh youse to had me git shud of hit, dese pockets is powerful venient foh weh I goes inter some ones house why I turns dose pockets wrong side out and dat always brings me good luck.

Mary contends that she always wears three petticoats.

"Marse Thamos lived in a big log house wid a big plantation all around hit. He had three hundred slaves on de two plantations. Marse Thamos sho was good ter us niggers. No nigger mus whoop his stock wid a switch. "I'se heared him say many time don't youse niggers whoop dese mules. How would you like to have me whoop you det way?" And he sho would whoop dem dem niggers if he cotched dem. Lawd have mercy who whould haw thot I'd be here all dis time. I'd thot I'd be ded and gone. All dese ole niggers try to be so uppity by jes bein raised in de house and cause dey was why dey think is Quality. Some of dese nigger gals was raised in de house but most of dem was made work ebery whar on de plantation. My Massa has his nigger gals to lay fence worms, mak fences, shuck corn, hoe corn en terbacco, wash, iron, and de missus try to teach de nigger gals to sew and knit. But shucks niggers aint got no sense nuf ter do fancy things. Sometimes I tended de chilluns.

"Yah, yah, I sho do member Abraham Lincoln. My Missus and Massa did not like Mr. Lincoln, but pshaw, all de niggers did. I member him, I seed him once, soon after I was freed.

"Pshaw, dey was hard times durin de war, my Missus and sum of de nigger gals and de chilluns hae to stay in the woods several days ter keep way from de soldiers. Dey eat all de chickens and kilt the cows and tuk de horses and we sho scairt out dar wid dem varmints roving roun.

"Nigger aint got no business being sot free, niggers still oughter be slaves. Us niggers did not hev to bother bout de victuals sor nuthin.

"Wen my Missis called us niggers gether and told us we was free I was as happy as a skinned frog but you seed I didn't have any sense. All niggers are fools. Now she says, she did, you can all stay here en work en we will pay you foh your work, or you can work foh some body else, but I hev raised you hones, and don't you steal, and work foh nuf money so you wont hev to steal it if youse gits hongry and haint got no money to buy vittals jus you ask de white folks foh hit and dey will giv hit to youse. Oh how I miss my Missis and Massa so much. Wish I hed dem now.

"Shucks on dese niggers and dar ways now. I lef de plantation my old Missus and Massa home and got on a steam boat on de Ohio Ribber and nursed de chillun foh de Captain and he's wife on dat boat foh about two year. An den He, He, He, a nigger don got much sense, Miss Fannie an Mr. Harry Campbell whot paid me foh my work on de boat gives Five Dollars foh de work en I'se didn't hev sense nuf ter know what ter do wid dis money. So I goes ter de store en buys me a cedar tub and filled hit wid candy. Miss Fannie gave me back de money foh de tub an den I ate nuf candy ter git sick and den Miss Fannie took de candy back to de store and she got my money back, she did.

"But shucks, I did not no whot ter do wid de money. Wen I lef Miss Fannie I rode to Henderson on a log raft en wen I got dar dey was a big circus and sum one was sayin, "de perade be here directly, He, He, He, I didn't no whot dey meant, big ignorant fool dat I was and still is, en wen I seed de elephants and de uther varmints I ran like a big pop-eyed fool nigger cause I never seed such things. Dat day on de road in town I met my ole Missus McElroy en she had me ter help her wid de chilluns and tuk me ter de circus and wen I got in de tent and saw all de cages and things I was sho scairt of ebery thing till I seed dem babboons dem I felt all right and at home cause I jes knowed dey was my first cousins. I stayed in Henderson foh sometime working foh furst one and tother en den Mr. Henry Shackleford hired me en brung me to Christian County. Not long fore I was married ter Albert Wooldridge we sho had a big wedding. Zack Major a nigger preacher of de Baptist faith did de ceremony right here in Hopkinsville.

"Yes, sho I has ben a mid-wife or granny. All dese high falutin things dey is doin now in child birth is tommy-rot dey oughter hev jes grannies now. I livered more babies den most doctors sometimes de white folks had doctors but I don't take no stock in dese doctors. De furst thing you does wen a new baby is born is ter let hit lay twenty minutes den cut de cord and dan grease a scortched rag wid lard jes hog lard en den put de belly band on den grease de baby all over. Neber wash de baby till tis over a week ole. Wen de babies had colic I'd take dirt dobber nest and make a tea, den giv did ter de baby. Sometimes If I couldn't fin no dirt dobber nes I would git a spider web and make a tea den giv dis or else jes shake de baby by de heels. If folks would tend ter babies like dey uster why dese people now wouldn't hev heart trouble.

"Sho I seed a ghost once, I soed Miss Annie Wooldridge after she died up here on Main St. I was jes settin on de back porch steps jes a lookin while da white folks was er eatin supper. Miss Annie allways got de eggs en I seed her dat day. She jes come thru de hen house door en hit was locked en den thru de pantry door and hit was locked en I jes called her daughter and I knowed I seed her, sho, I did, it who was Miss Annie.

"Of course dar is hanted houses. De ole Sharp house were dat er way and all de Sharps were ded but dis house were empty. You neber did see anything but I sho had heared de doors slam en de silver rattle en at night in my cabin near to hit I'd sees lights bob up en down. Any body in dis town can tell you dats so foh dey tore dis house down ter run de hants eraway.

"People don bother bout de moon much now but if dey would lissen ter de ole niters dey would always hev good crops. Now if you plant pertatoes by de dark of de moon you will always hev good crops en if you plant dem on de light of de moon den you hes all vine. Corn planted on de light de moon den you has a good crop. I'se knows cause I ken member fore de niggers wore freed you could jes plant by de moon and plant anything in God's ground en by de moon en de crops would grow. Now dey jes buther up God's ground en put ole stinky messy fertilizer on hit en de crops jes burn up. Nobody oughter mess wid God's ground.

"I'se a Publican who ever heared of a Democrat nigger. Nigger neber did own enything so dey cant be Democrats en if dey vote a Democrat ticket dey is jes votin a lie. Cause no nigger neber did own slaves only the old nigger slave traders and dey werent nuthin but varmints anyway. Ye jes has to hev owned slaves to vote a Democrat ticket en den no nigger eber did own slaves er hed nothing."

(Mary lives in Clarksville, Pike R.R. #1, Hopkinsville, Kentucky)

CALDWELL CO.
(MARY E. O'MALLEY) [HW: KY 6]

CALDWELL

Coal Mine Slaves: In 1836 large numbers of slaves were brought into Caldwell and worked by the owners of the ore mines, which necessitated extra patrols, interfered with local workmen, and so on. The taxpayers complained to the Legislature and an extra tax was allowed to be levied for the benefit of the county. In other books we find that the owners of the slaves who worked in these mines was President Andrew Jackson who brought his slaves from Nashville to the iron and lead mines in Caldwell and Crittenden counties; he is said to have made several trips himself to these mines.

The Missing Man:

"In 1860 Mr. Jess Stevens owned a negro slave, and his wife. Jess Williams, who lived in the north end of the county, bought the old slave, but did not buy his wife.

"One day one of Jess William's boys went to Edward Stevens and an argument followed, causing Mr. Stevens to shoot him in the arm. Later Jess Williams took the old negro and went to the field where Edward Stevens and the boy were planting corn. They hid behind a tree and the negro was given the gun and was told to shoot when Stevens came down the road by them.

"He came by slowly covering corn but the negro did not shoot. Williams said, "Why didn't you shoot?" and the negro replied, "Massie, I just didn't have da heart." Williams said, "If you don't shoot next time, I'm going to shoot you." When Stevens started by the negro shot and killed him, tearing his hoe handle into splinters.

One day a salesman, who rode a fine horse and had a beautiful saddle came to Princeton and later went to the Williams home. Several days later his people got anxious about him, and after checking up they found that he was last seen going into the Williams home. Several days later his people found his hat floating upon a pond near the house, and a few weeks later one of the Williams boys came to town riding the saddle that the salesman had ridden a few months before.

The old negro slave went to Mr. Stevens to visit his wife, and while he and Mr. Stevens were in the field a spy was hidden in the ambush listening to the conversation about the salesman. When the old slave returned home he was tied to the tail of a young mule, which was turned loose in a new ground and was dragged, bruised and almost killed. Edward Williams, son of Jess Williams, found the old slave and cut him loose. His father and brother found it out and started out to hunt him, intending to kill him, but he managed to dodge them.

Mr. Jess Stevens was walking along a path the next morning and heard a mournful groan, and after looking for awhile found the old slave. The worms had eaten his face[HW:?] and he was almost dead. The people brought him to the courthouse and began ringing the bell to let the people know that some injustice had been done. When one became tired another took his place. The bell rang both night and day until most of the citizens of the county came to see what was wrong. A number of men went in daytime, without mask or disguise, to the Williams home and hung Jess Williams. They intended to hang the two boys but they got away.

United States. Work Projects Administration

BALLARD CO.
(J.R. WILKERSON) [HW: KY 7]

[TINIE FORCE AND ELVIRA LEWIS:]

TINIE FORCE AND ELVIRA LEWIS

During the period of slavery in the Purchase Region, buying and selling slaves was carried on at irregular intervals. The trading usually took place at the home of the slave owner. The prices paid for slaves was dependent upon certain conditions. In case of a full grown, robust negro boy the price was sometimes as much as one thousand dollars. The prices paid was varied according to the age, the general health and other conditions of the individual.

At times pathetic scenes prevailed in the selling of slaves; namely, the separation of mother and child. Often, a boy or girl would be sold and taken away from his or her mother. In many cases the parting would be permanent and the child and its mother would never see each other again.

The slave owner maintained separate housing quarters for his slaves. In some cases the living quarters of slaves was comfortable and agreeable; in other cases, living conditions of slaves was anything but agreeable; Some masters were reasonably gentle to their slaves, while others were cruel.

One of the saddest, darkest and most pathetic conditions that existed during the period of slavery was the intimate mingling of slave owners, in fact many white men, with negro women. It has become known that very often a slave was sold who was the direct offspring of his or her owner. This practice prevailed to some extent in the Purchase Region, but was not universal. When the emancipation proclamation became effective and the slaves were given freedom, some of them prefered to remain with their masters, while others started out into the world for themselves. Very often, some of the slaves, who had anticipated that liberty meant more to them than anything else, and who went out into the cold world of indifference, soon returned to their old masters. They found that their former home was a much better place to abode than anything outside of it.

Recreations of slaves:

The following is an old fashion ballad that was sung during the period of slavery and which was very common throughout the Purchase Region: "Jeff Davis rode a big white horse, but Lincoln rode a mule—Jeff Davis was a fine, smart man, and Lincoln was a fool. Jeff Davis had a fine white; Lincoln only had a mule—Jeff Davis was a wonderful man and Lincoln was a fool".

Ring dancing was largely practiced during the slavery period. Especially was this participated in throughout the Purchase Region. This was a rather primative kind of dancing and was performed mostly by negro children. The general procedure was to draw a ring on the ground, ranging from 15 to 30 feet in diameter. The size of the ring to be used was determined by the number of persons who were engaged in the dancing ring. The youngsters would congregate within the ring and dance to the rhythmic hand clapping and rhythm of the tambourine, which was performed by the white people in the community.

Sometimes large congregations witnessed these primitive affairs, and they became a great Saturday evening entertainment for the community at large. During the periods of intermission, the youngsters, who had engaged in the dancing would be given a kind of feast on barbecued meat and cider drinking. At the conclusion of this brief festivity, they would continue in their dancing, and very often this hilarity would be carried on well into the evening.

Another kind of entertainment, which was practiced during the period of slavery, was the singing of negro folk songs and spirituals. The darkies would hold gatherings of this kind at the homes of individuals or members, and engage in singing their favorite songs. These singings were generally held during the evenings, especially on Saturdays and Sundays, and not only afforded a favorite pass time for the darkies; but also for white people. Most always, the singings were attended by a large audience of white people, men, women and children. Those gatherings grew with increasing popularity, until they became one of the most favorite classes of amusement.

Also, the darkies were very fond of sports, such as were

common to the period, and many of them were very dexterous in the leading sports of the day. One of the most common of those was hurdle racing. Here, the contestants would leap over hurdles that were placed at regular intervals apart. At time, numerous participants would engage in these races, and the sport would extend over the entire day. There was a kind of jumping too, which was called hurtling. In the sport, the contestants made use of a hurtling pole, which was a small rigid-pole about 12 feet in length. The jumper would take a long running start, which would enable him to take on additional momentum; and with the assistance of the hurtling pole, would leap over a hurdle that was placed a considerable elevation above the ground. The chief object in this kind of jumping was leaping over a high hurdle. The contestant, who made the highest leap, was awarded the highest honors of the contest. A second, third and fourth honors were awarded too.

Another kind of contest was called "A free for all". Here a ring was drawn on the ground which ranged from about 15 ft. to 30 ft. in diameter depending on the number of contestants who engaged in the combat. Each participant was given a kind of bag that was stuffed with cotton and rags into a very compact mass. When so stuffed, the bags would weigh on an average of 10 pounds, and was used by the contestants in striking their antagonist. Each combatant picked whichever opponent he desired and attempted to subdue him by pounding him over the head with the bag, which he used as his weapon of defense. And which was used as an offending weapon. The contest was continued in this manner till every combatant was counted out, and a hero of the contest proclaimed. Some times two contestants were adjudged heroes, and it was necessary to run a contest between the two combatants before a final hero could be proclaimed. Then the two antagonist would stage a battle royal and would continue in the conflict till one was proclaimed victorious.

Sometimes these Free-For-All battles were carried on with a kind of improvised boxing gloves, and the contests were carried on in the same manner as previously described. Very often, as many as 30 darkies of the most husky type were engaged in these battles, and the contests were generally attended by large audiences. Being staged during the period of favorable weather, and mostly on Saturday afternoon; these physical exhibitions were the scenes of much controversial conflict, gambling, excessive inebriation and hilarity.

Banjo and guitar playing were practiced by the many darkies of the slavery period also. These were on the order of concerts; and many darkies although they had no scientific training, became rather accomplished musicians in this respect. Melodious music might be heard at these old fashion contests, as most darkies, who acquired knowledge in the playing of these instruments were familiar with nearly all the melodies and folks songs that were common to the period.

(The foregoing is copied verbatim from conversation with Tinie Force, and Elvira Lewis, LaCenter, Ky. These 2 negro women are very familiar with the slavery period, as they were both slaves, and many of the facts common to that time were witnessed by them.)

United States. Work Projects Administration

LAWRENCE CO.
(EDNA LANE CARTER)

LAWRENCE

Extract from the Civil War diary kept by Elphas P. Hylton, a Lawrence Co. volunteer in the Union Army. "On 17th of July (1864) I was detailed for picket duty and saw three thousand negro soldiers on a grand review, a black cloud to see. On the 18th I was relieved of duty. Here I became dissatisfied as a soldier on account of the negro, negro, negro. On the 23rd we began to get ready to leave this negro hole and on the 24th, to our great joy and gladness, we were sent into camp near Danville."

United States. Work Projects Administration

LESLIE CO.
(VIOLA BOWLING)

LESLIE

McIntosh was a very progressive farmer and had a large supply of food, being a Rebel of the Rebel Army camped at the mouth of this creek near his home where they could secure food. He had a slave called "Henry McIntosh" who was drafted into the Union Army. He did not want to go but his master told him, "Well Henry you will have to go, do not steal, nor lie and be good and when you get out come on back." He did come back and stayed here until he died, he later married and was the father of "Ben McIntosh (colored) who later lived in Hyden for years. McIntosh did not have any help on his farm after this slave was taken away from him. So he let the youth of 16 years Mr. Wooton, come to his home and help him get wood and work about the place. McIntosh had another slave but gave him to his son-in-law John Hyden, who then lived one mile up Cutushin from the Mouth of McIntosh. He had a small store which was the first store in that community.

United States. Work Projects Administration

GARRARD CO.
(SUE HIGGINS)

GARRARD

Myth: Notions about nature when the stars fell in 1833.

At the Old Thomas Kennedy farm (Uncle Tom's Cabin), young Tom and some more boys were playing cards in one of the negro cabins. One of the slaves went to the cabin door and called loudly, "Mas'r Tom! Come quick, the whole heavens is falling." He continued to call. After much persuasion and repeated calls from the old negro, young Tom said, "I'll go and see what the D---- old negro wants". Young Tom went to the door and saw the stars raining down. He ran to the big house and jumped on a feather bed, and prayed loudly for help.

[Mrs. Jennie Slavin:]

When she was a child, Mrs. Slavin was our nearest neighbor. She said her father used to tell her these tales. William Kavanaugh was her father.

United States. Work Projects Administration

WEBSTER CO.
(J. DUNBAR)

WEBSTER

Slaves were brought and sold in Clay at one time. A large, stout negro woman in good health sold for $300 to $500. A large stout negro man sold for $1,000. Children were sold for $150 to $200. Mr. Tom Johnson, who is living now, states his father was a slave trader and was the chief sheriff of Webster Co. The runaway slaves were usually caught in this part of the country. The reward was usually $100.00.

United States. Work Projects Administration

CALDWELL CO.
(MARY E. O'MALLEY)

ESTHER HUDSPETH:

CALDWELL

The following story was given by a colored woman, Esther Hudespeth, who was once sold as a slave. It was told to her by her slave mother in 1840.

"A long time ago there lived a rabbit and a coon. They lived so close together. One morning Mr. Coon came by after Mr. Rabbit, and wanted him to go over to see some girls with him. So Mr. Rabbit agreed and went with Mr. Coon. Mr. Coon and the girls had some fun making fun of Mr. Rabbit's short tail. Mr. Rabbit was very glad when the time came for him to go home, because he was tired of being talked about. Mr. Coon had to go get a drink of water, and Mr. Rabbit told the girls that Mr. Coon was his riding horse and he would ride him when he came back. By the time he got thru telling the girls, Mr. Coon called to Mr. Rabbit that he was ready to go. Mr. Coon had enjoyed himself so much, while Mr. Rabbit had not.

The next day Mr. Coon came by for Mr. Rabbit to go with him to see the girls. Mr. Rabbit played sick. I am too sick to walk over there, he said. Mr. Coon said, I will carry you on my back if you want to ride. No, said Mr. Rabbit, I cant ride on your back. I will fall off.

Mr. Rabbit said, If you will let me put this saddle and bridle on you, I will go. So Mr. Coon agreed to let Mr. Rabbit put the saddle and bridle on Mr. Coon. So they went along thru the woods. When they got in sight of the House, Mr. Coon told Mr. Rabbit to get off—that he did not want the girls to see him on his back. Mr. Rabbit pulled out a whip and began to whip Mr. Coon, hollowing so the girls would see him, and made Mr. Coon go up to the hitching rack. There Mr. Rabbit hitched Mr. Coon and went in the house and enjoyed himself with the girls, while Mr. Coon pawed the ground. Mr. Rabbit bade the girls goodbye, and never did Mr. Coon come after Mr. Rabbit to go to see the girls with him.

**ANDERSON CO.
(MILDRED ROBERTS)**

ANDERSON

Many of the following stories were related by Mr. W.B. Morgan who at one time owned and operated a livery barn. He hired several negroes to look after the horses and hacks, and remembers many funny tales about them and others:

"Kie Coleman, one of my employees, was standing without the livery stable smoking a two-fer cigar that some one had given him. Another negro walked up to chat with him, and he reared back and said "Get away nigger, nothing but the rich can endure life."

"I was hauling grain for the distillery. One morning I came down to the barn, and Kie was too drunk to take his team out. I gave him a good going over about wasting his money that way instead of saving it for a decent funeral. This is one of the best ways to appeal to a darkey because if there is any thing they like it is a big funeral.

"He just kinda staggered up to me and said "Boss, I don't worry a bit about dat. White folks don't like to smell a live nigger and I'se knows good and well da hain't gwine to lebe no dead nigger laying on top of de groun'."

"I furnished the horses for the hearse, and one night I tole the boys to leave it in the stable because we were going to have another funeral the next day.

"Each night one of the boys had to sleep in the office, and this particular night it was Bill's turn. Bill was an old, one-legged negro and very superstitious. He said:

"Boss, this is my night to stay here, and you know, boss, I sho likes to work for you, but I jest tells you now there jest hain't room in this here house fer me and that black wagon at night." I moved the hearse."

KNOX CO.
(STEWART CAREY)

KNOX

Some slaves were owned in Knox Co., most of them being in Barbourville where they served as house-servants. The negro men worked around the house and garden, while the women were cooks and maids. The slaves usually lived in small one-room houses at the rear of their masters home, and were generally well fed and clothed.

There was some trading of slaves among the Barbourville and Knox County owners, and few were sold at Public Auction. These public sales were held on Courthouse Square, and some few slaves were bought and sold by "Negro Traders" who made a business of the traffic in blacks. Occasionally a negro man would be sold away from his family and sent away, never to see his people again.

United States. Work Projects Administration

CLARK CO.
(MAYME NUNNELLEY)

CLARK

Most Kentucky superstitions are common to all classes of people because the negroes originally obtained most of their superstitions from the white and because the superstitions of most part of Kentucky are in almost all cases not recent invention but old survivals from a time when they were generally accepted by all germanic peoples and by all Indo-Europeans.

The only class of original contributions made by the negroes to our stock of superstitions is that of the hoodoo or voodoo signs which are brought from Africa by the ancestors of the present colored people of America. On the arrival of the negro in America, his child like mind was readily receptive to the white man's superstitions.

The Black slave and servants in Kentucky and elsewhere in the South have frequently been the agents through which the minds of white children have been sown with these supernatural beliefs, some of which have remained permanently with them. Nearly all classes of superstitions find acceptance among the negroes. The most widely prevalent are beliefs concerning haunted houses, weather signs, bad luck and good luck signs, charm curse and cures and hoodoo signs. Their beliefs that the date of the planting of vegetables should be determined by the phases of the moon is unshaken.

CASEY CO.
(R.L. NESBITT)

CASEY

While slavery existed in Casey Co., as in other counties of the State, before the Civil War, there are no negroes living the the county today who were born into slavery; and very few white people who can remember customs, incidents, or stories of the old slavery days. It is known that the first slaves in the county were those brought here from Virginia by the early white settlers of the county; and that until they were given their freedom, the slaves were well cared for and kindly treated. They lived in comfortable cabins on the lands of their owners, well fed and clothed, given the rudiments of spiritual and educational training, necessary medical attention in sickness; and it was not unusual for some slave owners to give a slave his or her freedom as a reward for faithful or unusual services. If there was any of the so-called "Underground Railway" method used to get slaves out of the state, as was the case in many counties, there are no current stories or legends relative to such to be heard in the county today. It is thought that the slaves of Casey County were so well cared for and so faithful and loyal to their masters that very few of them cared to leave and go to non-slavery states in the North. So there was little, if any, call for any secret methods to provide for their escape. Even after they were given their freedom, many slaves refused to leave their masters and spent the remainder of their lives in the service and as charges of their former owners. The present generation of course knows nothing of slavery, and even the older people know only what was told them by the forebears, and no especially interesting stories or legends are current in the county today relative to slaves, or the customs of the old slavery days before the War between the States.

CHRISTIAN CO.
(MAMIE HANBERY)

CHRISTIAN

HOO-DOOISM

A snake head an' er lizard tail, Hoo-doo;
Not close den a mile o' jail, Hoo-doo;
De snake mus' be er rattlin' one,
Mus' be killed at set uv sun,
But never while he's on de run, Hoo-doo.

Before you get de lizard cot, Hoo-doo;
You mus' kill it on de spot, Hoo-doo;
Take de tail an' hang it up,
Ketch de blood in a copper cup,
An' be sure it's uv a pup, Hoo-doo.

Wait until sum stormy weather, Hoo-doo;
Put de head an' feet together, Hoo-doo;
In a dry ol' terrapin shell,
Let 'em stay fer a good long spell,
But don't you ever try to sell, Hoo-doo.

De rattlers mus' be jus' seben, Hoo-doo;
But mus' not be ober leben, Hoo-doo;
He mus' be curl'd up fix'd to fight,
But see dat you don' let him bite,
Den you hit w'en de time is right, Hoo-doo.

Ef you do, it's power is dead, Hoo-doo;
'Cause it is all right in de head, Hoo-doo;
Save de head and de buttons, too,
Fer de work you'll have ter do,
You will need 'em till you're thru, Hoo-doo.

Ketch a live scorpen wid you han', Hoo-doo;
Drown in mare's milk in a pan, Hoo-doo;
Den dry it on a pure lime rock,
Ninety-nine minutes by de clock, Hoo-doo.

Den git a hand which is a bag, Hoo-doo;
Made uv any sort uv rag, Hoo-doo;
An' let de top be color'd blue,
Den git de hair frum out de shoe, Hoo-doo.

Now we'n you find de folks ain't well, Hoo-doo;
An' dey wants you to move de spell, Hoo-doo;
Git your gredients together,
Ster dem up wid a goose feather,
In sum dark an' cloudy weather, Hoo-doo.

Den put 'em in de hoo-doo bag, Hoo-doo;
In dat little blue top rag, Hoo-doo;
Den slip 'em in between de ticks,
Ef you want de conjure fixed,
Is de way you do de tricks, Hoo-doo.

Ef dey wants you to git 'em well, Hoo-doo;
Dat is de han' dat moves de spell, Hoo-doo;
Take it out before der eyes,
An' you mus' be awful s'prised,

And dey will think dat you is wise, Hoo-doo.

Den lay right down on your back, Hoo-doo;
Ef you hear de timbers crack, Hoo-doo;
Den yer kno's yer trick has won,
Den you'll ast er-bout de mon,
For you kno's yer work is done, Hoo-doo.

Now ef you wants de conjure fixt, Hoo-doo;
All you do is to turn de tricks, Hoo-doo;
Jes git dat bottle what you had,
An' to make your patient glad,
Is but to make de conjurer mad, Hoo-doo.

United States. Work Projects Administration

HOPKINS CO.
(M. HANBERRY)

HOPKINS

[TR: also spelled Hanbery.]

In this county practically no one owned more than one or two slaves as this was never a county of large plantations and large homes. These slaves were well housed, in cabins, well clothed and well fed, not overworked and seldom sold, were in closer touch with the "white folks" and therefore more intelligent than farther south where slaves lived in quarters and seldom came in contact with their masters or the masters' families. When a gentleman wished a slave he usually went to Hopkinsville and bought slaves there. Occasionally one slave owner would buy one from another. "If there was ever a slave market in Madisonville or Hopkins County I do not remember it or ever heard of it," says J.M. Adams, book-keeper of Harlen Coal Company, age 84, Madisonville, Ky.

United States. Work Projects Administration

MARTIN CO.
(CULLEN JUDE)

MARTIN

In the year 1864, during the conflict between the North and South, a new citizen was added to the town of Warfield. His name was Alfred Richardson, a colored man. Heretofore the people would not permit negroes to live in Warfield.

Richardson was in a skirmish at Warfield and was listed among the northern people as missing. His leg was injured and he was in a serious condition. The good people living at Warfield had their sympathies stirred up by his condition and took him in and gave him food and medical attention until he was able to work.

At first the people thought they had done a Samaritan Act, but as soon as Alf had a chance to prove himself, he was considered a blessing and not a curse. He became the paper hanger for the town. Then someone wanted to have his hair cut and Alf proved to be an excellent barber.

He rented a shop and went into the barber business and made a success. He owned considerable land, and other property when he died. He lived and died at Warfield, Ky., and was considered one of its most up to date citizens.

www.ingramcontent.com/pod-product-compliance
Lightning Source LLC
Chambersburg PA
CBHW061259110426
42742CB00012BA/1975